THE LIGHT OF GRACE

Also by Sirshree

Spiritual Masterpieces - Self Realisation books for serious seekers

Who Am I Now: From mindfulness to no-mind
Answers that Awaken: Access the Source of Wisdom within You
100% Karma: Learn the Art of Conscious Karma that Liberates
100% Wisdom: Wisdom that leads you to experience and be established in your true nature
100% Meditation: Dip into the Stillness of Pure Awareness
You are Meditation: Discover Peace and Bliss Within
Essence of Devotion: From Devotee to Divinity
The Unshaken Mind: Discovering the Purpose, Power and Potential of your mind
The Supreme Quest: Your search for the Truth ends there where you are
The Greatest Freedom: Discover the key to an Awakened Living
Secret of The Third Side of The Coin: Unravelling Missing Links in Spirituality
Seek Forgiveness & be Free: Liberation from Karmic Bondage
Passwords to a Happy Life: The Art of Being Happy in all Situations

Self Help Treasures - Self Development books for success seekers

The Source of Health: The Key to Perfect Health Discovery
Inner Ninety Hidden Infinity: How to build your book of values
Inner 90 for Youth: The secret of reaching and staying at the peak of success
The Source for Youth: You have the power to change your life
Inner Magic: The Power of self-talk
Self Encounter: The Complete Path - Self Development to Self Realization
The Five Supreme Secrets of Life: Unveiling the Ways to Attain Wealth, Love and God
You are Not Lazy: A story of shifting from Laziness to Success
Freedom From Fear, Worry, Anger: How to be cool, calm and courageous
The Little Gita of Problem Solving: Gift of 18 Solutions to Any Problem
Freedom From Failure: 7 Spiritual Secrets That Transform Failure Into A Blessing

New Age Nuggets - Practical books on applied spirituality and self help

The Source: Power of Happy Thoughts
Secret of Happiness: Instant Happiness - Here and Now!
Excuse me God...: Fulfilling your wishes through the Power of Prayer and Seed of Faith
Help God to Help You: Whatever you do, do it with a smile
Ultimate Purpose of Success: Achieving Success in all five aspects of life
Celebrating Relationships: Bringing Love, Life, Laughter in Your Relations
Everything is a Game of Beliefs: Understanding is the Whole Thing
Detachment From Attachment: Gift of Freedom From Suffering
Emotional Freedom Through Spiritual Wisdom: How to Take Charge of Your Emotions

Profound Parables - Fiction books containing profound truths

Beyond Life: Conversations on Life After Death
The One Above: What if God was your neighbour?
The Warrior's Mirror: The Path To Peace
Master of Siddhartha: Revealing the Truth of Life and After-life
Put Stress to Rest: Utilizing Stress to Make Progress
The Source @ Work: A Story of Inspiration from Jeeodee

Author of the bestseller *The Source*

SIRSHREE

THE LIGHT OF GRACE

Why Guru, God, Grace and You are one

The Light of Grace
Why Guru, God, Grace and You are One
By Sirshree Tejparkhi

Copyright © Tejgyan Global Foundation
All Rights Reserved 2018

Tejgyan Global Foundation is a charitable organization
with its headquarters in Pune, India.

Published by WOW Publishings Pvt. Ltd., India

First edition published in July 2018

Printed and bound by Repro India Limited

Copyrights are reserved with Tejgyan Global Foundation and publishing rights are vested exclusively with WOW Publishings Pvt. Ltd. This book is sold subject to the condition that it shall not by way of trade or otherwise, be lent, resold, hired out, or otherwise circulated without the publisher's prior written consent in any form of binding or cover other than that in which it is published and without a similar condition including this condition being imposed on the subsequent purchaser and without limiting the rights under copyright reserved above, no part of this publication may be reproduced, stored in or introduced into a retrieval system, or transmitted, in any form, or by any means, electronic, mechanical, photocopying, recording or otherwise, without the prior written permission of both the copyright owner and the above-mentioned publisher of this book. Any person who does any unauthorized act in relation to this publication may be liable to criminal prosecution and civil claims for damages.

*To those seekers
whose sole purpose of life
is to attain the true Self,
to be established in it and
to express its divine qualities
through their body-minds;
to serve for the wellbeing of humanity;
to be instrumental for spreading
the divine wisdom of the Self.*

Editor's Note

This book is a compilation of discourses and question-answer sessions with Sirshree that discuss the Guru principle, how it functions through the body-mind of the guru. It is presented in the form of conversations between Sirshree and seekers of the truth.

Seekers who come from diverse backgrounds gather for a series of discussion sessions with Sirshree to share their life situations and gain clarity. These conversations happen between designated seekers A and B, who converse with Sirshree.

Although Sirshree enacts the role of guru, when he speaks about the guru, he is speaking from an impersonal standpoint without any identification with the role of the Guru. Also, the mention of "he" or "him" to refer to the guru is only for the convenience of usage of language. In all such instances, the reader should interpret it gender-agnostically as "he" or "she". This is because the true guru is beyond gender.

The reader is encouraged to read these conversations sequentially, so as to benefit from the systematic unraveling of understanding.

Contents

Preface		9
1.	Importance of the Guru	13
2.	What is a True Guru?	19
3.	Discerning the Guru's Authenticity	27
4.	Grace is the Only Way	40
5.	The Need and Urgency for Self-Realization	49
6.	Transcending the Body-Mind Temperaments	56
7.	Role of the Guru	69
8.	The State of Complete Surrender	80
9.	The Paths Leading to the Truth	86
10.	Significance of the Guru-Disciple Relationship	98
11.	Training the Body, Mind and Intellect	106
12.	The Guru's Attention	114
13.	Qualities of the Truth-Seeker	120

14. Common Mistakes of the Disciple	125
15. Same Questions, Changing Answers	132
16. Teaching, Training and Testing	136
Addendum: The Significance of Guru Purnima	142

Preface

Many a time, we watch channels like Discovery or Animal Planet, which raise awareness about the species of plants and animals that are on the verge of extinction. Experts from all over the world work unanimously towards preserving them. They create controlled, conducive environments and sanctuaries for such species to breed in. Thus, there is a conscious effort to preserve whatever is supposed to be invaluable.

If so much effort is being invested to save animals and plants from extinction, the question arises whether we are putting in similar efforts to preserve the divine wisdom that helps us attain the true purpose of our lives?

Self-realized sages devised various ways of passing on this wisdom through generations. However, with the passage of time, the underlying essence has been lost and the means has become the end in itself. People believe that they can attain God just by following certain spiritual practices or rituals. Hence, with time, the essence of spirituality has been lost.

Now, the time has come to revive the spiritual essence. For this, one needs a true guru, who has attained the ultimate purpose of life and imparts divine wisdom in contemporary language to help others attain the same.

In this age, where there are numerous so-called schools of spirituality and varied disciplines, it is becoming increasingly difficult for an earnest seeker of truth to determine an authentic guru who can guide him on the path. How does a seeker differentiate the genuine from imitations? It is this dilemma that is set to rest through this book that expounds what the true Guru essence is. It throws light on the way of working of a true guru and how a sincere disciple can truly benefit from the presence of the Guru.

This book systematically explains the current scenario of spiritual pursuit, various kind of practices being followed in the name of spirituality, the importance of a true guru, the need and urgency of Self-realization, different paths that lead to the same goal, the nature of the body-mind of the seeker and its necessary training, the required qualities to walk on this path, to name a few.

With the divine wisdom received from the guru, the seeker learns to practice *sadhana* in the midst of worldly activities to annihilate his ego and be established in the experience of the true Self. It's only with the light of grace of the true guru that the seeker attains the ultimate truth. He then realizes that God, Guru, Grace and the real "I" are one and the same. The truth that he was seeking outside, resides within him.

It becomes clear to him that the formless essence of the guru has always been guiding him from within since the very beginning. The external guru helps him get rid of his ignorance. Thereafter, immersed in the feeling of devotion and gratitude, he unleashes his latent potential and expresses the divine qualities of the Self. His life becomes a celebration of truth in itself!

Hope this book serves as a torch of wisdom in your search for the truth and awakens the guru within you.

1
Importance of the Guru

Seekers who come from diverse backgrounds have gathered for a series of discussion sessions with Sirshree to share their life situations and gain clarity. Two designated seekers A and B converse with Sirshree. The reader is encouraged to read these conversations sequentially, so as to benefit from the systematic unraveling of understanding.

Seeker A: Today about half the world's population practices some form of monotheism. They believe in a singular God. The rest believe in multiple Gods, a form of polytheism. Is it essential to worship a form of God? Was there any purpose behind having multiple forms of God?

Sirshree: Let's understand why different forms of God came into existence in the first place. Self-realized sages from ancient times realized the need for the surrender of the human mind and ego for the sake of spiritual progress. Additionally, if one were to imbibe divine qualities such as love, joy, peace, compassion, purity, courage, devotion, etc. …to name a few, then one would excel in one's spiritual practice by leaps and bounds. Further, it was essential to pass on the knowledge of truth to further generations. Hence, they devised different forms of God as a medium to serve this purpose. They also setup a custom of worshipping these forms. These different forms symbolize God.

Seeker A: I understood the purpose of having forms of God; that they are symbolic representations. But, I'm unable to understand why there are so many forms. Is there any specific reason?

Sirshree: The reason behind having multiple forms of God was to personify the abstract principles of natural laws and vital forces of the nature. The *Shiv-linga* has been conceived by Self-realized sages to represent the original state of Self-in-rest when the world was not manifested. It is the state of nothingness which has also been known as *Shunya-murti* – *Shunya* meaning Zero or Nothingness. The idol symbolizing the *Nataraja* (dance of lord Shiva), symbolizes the coming into action of the Self, leading to manifestation of the world. The cycle of creation, maintenance and destruction is being perpetuated in the universe. This has been symbolized by the trinity of *Brahma, Vishnu and Mahesh* in India. Thus, different idols symbolize different aspects of God.

Seeker A: This is simply marvelous! I never thought there is so much insight in all of this. Definitely there had to be some reason behind worshipping these forms as well.

Sirshree: Yes. Once the knowledge of the truth was encoded in the form of idols, there was a need to decode and imbibe the personified qualities in one's life. The custom of worshipping of idols came into place so as to encourage people to contemplate on these idols to reveal those symbolic secrets held within them. It was ensured that the custom gets passed on from generation to generation so that future generations also get the same results.

Seeker A: Okay. I can now see that there has been a profound thought that has been given to conceiving these idols of God. But, what exactly happens when one worships such forms?

Sirshree: When one worships the form, he in turn contemplates upon the essential nature that the idol embodies and realizes this nature at the level of experience. The idol then becomes God in a true sense, rather than be a mere statue. By seeing God in one idol, the possibility of seeing God in all beings rises.

When one contemplates upon the divine qualities of the idol, those qualities get imbibed and activated within him. He then starts experiencing the same truth within himself and becomes instrumental for the expression of the true Self.

Seeker B: Is this somehow linked with the Indian mythological belief that there are thirty-three million Gods?

Sirshree: Consider an idea that the population of the Indian subcontinent was thirty-three million at that time. But now the population has increased, so people need to revise this number. The idea was to see the presence of God within every being.

Seeker B: Can I then worship a single idol instead of so many?

Sirshree: The number doesn't matter here. The idol, which helps one dissolve one's ego, is a sacred idol. If one finds it easier to surrender unto a rounded stone which symbolizes zero or nothingness, one may do so. The important part here is people should learn to surrender. It can be any idol, or guru or a formless presence, in front of which one finds it easier to surrender.

Seeker A: But what if the mind doesn't surrender?

Sirshree: The ego likes to maintain its separate existence. Hence, it refuses to surrender.

Seeker B: Whenever I worship, I find myself preoccupied with lots of thoughts about the past and the future. At such times, I read some scriptures and find solace. But the next day the same thing repeats.

Sirshree: The scriptures can be of help to a certain point. You can read the scriptures as many times as you want. But, the scriptures can't question you, "Did you contemplate on what you read earlier?"

It is important to surrender the ego. Unto whom you surrender is immaterial. When the ego doesn't want to surrender, an idol or the scriptures won't counter it, but a living guru can. That's the significance of a living guru.

A contemporary, living guru can ask you, "What happened to the commitments you made yesterday?" He will demand answers from you. He will awaken you, destroy your ego and make you witness the play of the ego in a detached way. It is therefore said that if ego is a disease, the guru is its doctor. His words, his silence, his instructions and his service work like a remedy.

Seeker B: How does a living guru destroy the ego?

Sirshree: It is in the nature of man that whenever he becomes a little knowledgeable, he becomes egoistic. As a result, he wants to highlight himself wherever he goes, which soon becomes the cause of his downfall. The ego declares, "Whatever knowledge I acquired is all because of my hard work." In reality, whenever the ego surrenders itself at the feet of the guru, only then does one become truly eligible for the truth. This understanding will immensely help you in freeing yourself from the ego.

Unless the ego is destroyed, the truth can't reveal itself. Idols of God have been created in order to surrender this ego. The ego needs to realize that it is a hurdle in the experience of the truth. A person is searching for God in the temple and enquiring, "Where is God? I've searched him all around here. I can't find him." He will be told, "God is standing right behind you, but is hidden because you are standing tall. You only need to bend low and bow down, and He will be revealed."

It is to destroy this ego that a living guru is required. When ego arises within you, the guru counters it and forces it to surrender. As soon as the one who believes himself to be separate from the rest surrenders, the truth is revealed. This is why the presence of a living guru is so important. But for this, sincere faith on the guru is very essential, because sincere faith enables one to surrender oneself completely. The feeling of total acceptance arises in the presence of the guru, which in turn facilitates the surrendering of the ego.

Seeker A: I have a basic question – how to identify the ego? When I am angry, does it mean that my ego is functioning?

Sirshree: Arrogance and anger both are just like two wild animals living in the same cave; the only difference is that anger is black, while arrogance is white. White does not appear to be as bad as black, because arrogance is subtler than anger. A person's anger is clearly perceptible, but ego or arrogance remains hidden.

The human ego is akin to icebergs on water. Although, they are made up of water, they have a separate existence of their own. They always want to stay above the surface of the expanse and stand out distinctly. In the same way, the human ego wants to stay separate from others.

Seeker A: If the ego can surrender in the presence of the guru, I would like to understand more about the guru.

Seeker B: Yes, I have a lot of apprehensions about this whole idea of a guru. Would like to understand more...

2
What is a True Guru?

Seeker B: What does the word "Guru" mean in the first place?

Sirshree: The word "Guru" is made up of two syllables – "Gu" and "Ru". "Gu" means darkness and "Ru" means light. Hence, Guru means one who dispels the darkness of ignorance, delusion, false notions and beliefs within us and lights the flame of wisdom.

Seeker A: I never thought the word "Guru" has such a profound meaning. But is it essential to have a guru? Can't we find our own way in life?

Sirshree: Is it essential to have a mother?

Seeker A: Definitely, how can we survive without a mother? At least at infancy, we need the loving care of the mother.

Sirshree: There are some children who grow up without mothers. Their mothers died at their birth or at some other time during their formative years. Yet they grow; they live. They appear just fine without a mother. However, some of these children have to go through lot of hardships in their life and those experiences make them bitter.

However, those who are nurtured by their mothers understand what unconditional love is and also understand why the mother is essential in life. So is it with the guru. Unless one is blessed with the grace of the guru, one doesn't understand the necessity of having a guru.

Seeker A: But there are millions of people whose lives have a purpose. They are engaged in creating something and have a role to play on this planet. It's not that without a guru, life is meaningless. There is still a meaning, still a sense to life.

Sirshree: Without a guru, life will not be meaningless; but it will be less meaningful. Those who lead their lives without a guru remain content with very little. They can't live even an inch of their life in a precise way. But, those who are willing to explore all the possibilities of their life must have a guru to lead them.

There are a few individuals who didn't have a guru and yet have attained the ultimate state of Self-realization; for example, Guru Nanak, Ramana Maharshi, Gautama Buddha. While they didn't have masters in their lives, they attained Self-realization on their own.

These individuals represent the exceptions. In most cases, a guru is required. Saint Tukaram, Saint Dnyaneshwar, Saint Meera, Saint Eknath, Saint Kabir, and many others belong to the list of those who had gurus. The reason is that for the truth to manifest, the judgmental and programmed mind has to drop, or step aside. The mind can't do this by itself. It is necessary to have faith in someone or something else.

Seeker B: When I was a child, I have been told by my parents that this particular person is our guru. We are not supposed to approach anyone else or attend any other discourses. If we do so, we are being a traitor.

Sirshree: There are many who are caught up in this confusion. People live their lives with this fear of being rejected. However, the truth is that the guru is not a specific person, a particular individual, or some body. The true guru is Consciousness within all, which is all-pervading.

Seeker A: If no body or no individual is a guru then whom should we regard as the guru?

Sirshree: The Consciousness within each one of us is the true guru. Thus, the Guru, in essence, is the life principle. It is Consciousness that has awakened to its own self. When it manifests completely in a body, that body plays the role of the guru. It is through this body that Self-realization happens and then the body reveals these profound secrets to you.

The Consciousness within you that is yet to be revealed is the guru. It is that Consciousness that guides you. It may guide you through a person, a book, or a dream. If required, the Consciousness can come into your life and awaken you in the form of an individual. If the Consciousness wants to manifest on its own, that too can happen. You can get guidance even through dreams.

Seeker B: If the guru can guide me through so many different forms, how can I receive the guidance?

Sirshree: For that, you need to keep yourself open and receptive. Do not close yourself saying that if one can attain

Self-realization on his own, then I too shall. That is not in your hands. Just be open and let Consciousness guide you the way it wants.

Seeker A: Then how do I identify my guru? How would he appear?

Sirshree: Usually people go by external appearance. They hold various beliefs about the guru, like: his head should be shaved, he should have dense long beard, he should hold beads of rosary in his hands, he should wear saffron or any special type of attire, he should make miracles out of sacred ash, he should solve all worldly problems.

However, if you are searching for a guru backed by these beliefs then you are seeking in the wrong direction. It will not lead you to God-realization. The earlier you free yourself from such beliefs, the better it would be. Otherwise, if you have the belief that the guru should walk on water, then a duck can be your guru. If you believe that the guru should fly in the sky, then a crow can be your guru. If someone can become your guru just by giving up his clothing, then a monkey would be the first one to attain Self-realization. External appearance is not the criterion to determine the true guru

Seeker B: Then how can a true guru be recognized? Should he be able to recite verses from ancient scriptures?

Sirshree: Many people believe that the guru should recite verses from Sanskrit scriptures, he should narrate mythological stories. In the spiritual congregation, worship and prayers should be performed, holy *Prasad* should be distributed. A seeker who is driven by such beliefs gets stuck in the costumes, hair makeover, and vocabulary used by the guru and remains deprived of the true knowledge of the Self.

A true guru is effective. When you listen to an effective guru, your life gets transformed. He is stabilized in the experience of the Self and guides each one as per their body-mind disposition. He has perfect understanding of the need of the times. He knows what's going on around him, what are the beliefs and illusions that people are entangled in. Accordingly, he gives examples in his discourses and guides people in today's prevalent language. To make things easier and simpler to understand, he may use filmy stories as analogies in his discourses.

Seeker B: Filmy stories in discourses?!

Sirshree: Have you ever had ice cream candy?

Seeker B: I had many since my childhood.

Sirshree: Then bring those sticks.

Seeker B: How can I bring them now? I already threw them after use.

Sirshree: The same is the case with words. Words are like the stick that holds the candy. Words convey the knowledge of truth. When you have had the candy, you throw away the stick. Nobody bothers about how the stick is. Similarly, whether the knowledge of truth is imparted in Sanskrit or today's local language, using mythological stories or today's filmy stories, it doesn't matter. The important thing is that the truth should be conveyed to the seeker and he should benefit from it.

This wisdom of truth is not new. It is eternal. It is there since ancient times. The earnest seeker of truth should have unbroken faith, a deep recognition of the guru from the heart, unconditional love towards the guru's instructions in addition to being unhesitatingly truthful. Deceit, distrust and assumptions pose hurdles in the attainment of truth. Therefore, he should burn all his assumptions and distrust in the fire of wisdom at the earliest.

The guru gives instant answers to the questions that emerge from a pure and thirsty heart of a truth seeker. When the guru counters the seeker in order to test him, the seeker should keep patience. He should provide an honest update to the guru about his progress and assumptions in his *sadhana*, spiritual practice.

Seeker A: But each seeker is different. How does the guru guide each of them differently?

Sirshree: You can understand this with the help of an example. Imagine that there are few people who want to reach the terrace of a building with transparent walls. The one who reaches at the top on the terrace can clearly see where the rest are and can guide them accordingly. In the same way, the guru has reached the terrace of being established in the experience of the true Self and can hence guide each seeker on their spiritual path. He exactly knows which things accelerate the seeker in their spiritual journey and guides them accordingly.

Seeker B: I am still not fully convinced about how I can recognize a true guru. Your "deep recognition of the guru from the heart" point has struck a chord in my heart. Can something happen to me internally when I come in contact with a true guru?

Sirshree: (laughs) In the presence of the true guru, your mind calms down and its habit of vacillating in thoughts subsides. The true guru will lead you towards the thoughtless state – the state beyond thoughts. His presence brings you the remembrance of who-you-truly-are; he safeguards you from the clutches of illusion, eradicates the fear of death from your mind and shatters all your wrong beliefs and notions. Know him alone to be the true guru.

Man is deceitful. He hides something according to his convenience. He may magnify or highlight something else to his benefit. He spins yarns or does not say some things directly. He gets into the habit of lying. There is no harmony between his feelings, thoughts, speech and action.

Where you become free of deceit, understand the value of truth, experience unconditional love and unbroken peace, understand that there is your final guru. He will lead you towards Self-realization and Self-stabilization. In fact, the guru is the one in whose presence you start shifting to the "no-mind" state.

Seeker A: Do you mean to say that when I will come in contact with a true guru, I will not remain the way I am?

Sirshree: Right. When a piece of iron comes in contact with a philosopher stone, it turns into gold. Once you are in contact with your true guru, his teachings become a part of your life. Your life gets transformed and you experience eternal bliss, peace and love.

Seeker A: But off late, I have been entertaining so many negative thoughts. How can I suddenly become so peaceful and blissful?

Sirshree: This does not happen overnight. But at least you begin to get the right direction for your spiritual journey. As you practice *sadhana* by following the teachings of your guru, you develop an eye to identify the wrong or right seeds you are sowing day and night in the form of your thoughts. Thereafter, you stop sowing wrong seeds. Whatever wrong seeds you have already sown, you nullify them with the help of the guru.

The guru develops infallible faith within you, which God wants from you. Once, you work in accordance with what God wants, you remain in harmony with God and become successful in a true sense. In that sense, the guru acts like a bridge between you and God. Thus, the possibility of you becoming more peaceful and blissful opens up. You need to practice and experience it to believe it. That's where the role of unswerving faith comes into picture.

Otherwise, you get in the hands of wrong so-called gurus who give you temporary relief. If not that, you incessantly chase after acquiring name, fame, designation, recognition and wealth. Instead of chasing after these things, it is important to stay connected with God. When you begin to live according to the real purpose of your life, your life becomes simple, straightforward, and yet powerful.

3
Discerning the Guru's Authenticity

Seeker A: I am fed up of all false gurus. The internet and news bulletins are rampant with stories related to fake gurus involved in money scams and various scandals.

Seeker B: Many of them appear to be noble in their cause in the beginning, but later on they are found involved in scams. Some join political parties and get elected. Some even encash their popularity and run big businesses in the name of healthcare and wellbeing. How can such immoral people pose as Gurus?

Seeker A: I am really scared of regarding someone as my guru. Whenever I think of a guru, I always feel that he should be a pure soul who is guiding me in my life. But I feel it's impossible to find someone like this in today's world. I don't want to risk my life by trusting someone as a guru.

Sirshree: Because of these so-called gurus, people have lost trust in the age old guru-disciple tradition. It is essential to know about these fake gurus so that you get the eye to assess a true guru. One can claim to be a guru under many guises, but a true guru is beyond all such claims.

Seeker A: What sort of claims?

Sirshree: So-called gurus self-proclaim themselves based on various claims.

Some claim to be a guru by healing disease using alternative therapies, by training people to use breath-work, by practising karmic rituals, or by claiming to awaken the *Kunadalini*.

Seeker A: I have heard about faith healers. They are more popular in Christianity. Their prayers help people release their faith and attain good health.

Sirshree: There is nothing wrong with approaching healers to bring physical and mental health. But one should not stop there. The human body in itself is a miracle. There are several points in our body that if tapped properly can help us attain good health. This is exactly what healers help people achieve. They religiously study such healing techniques and help rid people of physical disease.

Seeker B: I've known of such teachers who impart techniques related to watching breath, vibrations, or light to their disciples. They ask their disciples to chant mantras a million times, meditate on the *chakras* of the energy-body, or awaken the Kundalini power within them for spiritual growth.

Sirshree: Mystical experiences and psychic abilities are sold in the name of spirituality! It is one thing to be curious about these occult practices but when these are categorized as "spiritual practices", then the real purpose of spirituality is lost.

These practices may have their own benefits. They may possibly help in healing traumas and serve as alternative therapies for body ailments. However, they deal at the plane of the human psyche, the plane of energy, or the physical body. True spirituality is beyond the mind, beyond the realm of energies, and beyond the physical realm. Hence, no amount of dabbling with these practices can ever lead one to the purpose of true spirituality. Instead, one's ego gets inflated in the process and he drifts farther from the true Self.

Seeker A: Indeed, people are made to undergo rituals in the name of spiritual cleansing with lofty promises of salvation. As you said, spirituality has been corrupted due to misguidance.

Seeker B: I have also known of priests who force people to follow them by scaring, threatening or even enticing them with bribes or false karmic rituals. They create an aura around them, as if they are gurus. They claim to change one's fortune if one performs their suggested ritual, or changes the name of one's shop, TV serial or film to start with one's lucky letter. I always doubted how changing a name can make so much difference.

Seeker A: I had been to Varanasi with my family to perform the last rites for my grandfather. There, the priests who perform the rituals for the dead were haggling for a good sum of money by offering ritual packages. Some were even posing as agents to send gifts for our deceased relatives so that they are taken care of in their afterlife!

Sirshree: Do you believe that the deceased ones really need such things there?

Seeker A: It is so absurd. I also wonder what the deceased one has to do with food, or shawls or sweaters when they have left behind their physical body on earth. Would they feel cold or hungry there?

Sirshree: (laughs) Such physical gifts are needed for the physical body here; they are no longer useful after the death of the physical body. Such rituals can help people here to get rid of their guilt or incompleteness. These rituals also feed the needs of the karmic gurus who receive these offerings for themselves!

Seeker B: I can see that these practices are distractions from the real goal of attaining the transcendent truth. Instead of bringing clarity, they only promote superstitions and bloat the ego.

Sirshree: A sincere truth seeker desires to get rid of his ego on the path of truth. But such practices do not lead him to liberation. Hence, he needs a true guru who can impart him the knowledge of the truth beyond such limiting beliefs and helps free him from such distractions.

Seeker A: I agree.

Sirshree: There are some who claim to be a guru by their attire. They shave their head, or keep a long beard, smear ashes on their forehead, wear garlands and chant mantras. Innocent people follow them out of blind faith and fall victim. These appearances don't bring any transformation in the lives of people. As a result, they remain deprived of the real truth.

Seeker B: They are frauds. They only imitate the dressing but their core is hollow.

Sirshree: There are also some who claim to be a guru by imparting a mantra to their followers. They travel from one place to another, share some mantra with the people and initiate them as their disciples. They then instruct these disciples to repeat the mantra throughout their lives.

Seeker B: Can recitation of such mantras help in attaining salvation?

Sirshree: It's true that mantras play a certain role in human life and their repetition yields some benefit. Your mind calms down with their repetition. However, such benefits are only temporary. You won't attain salvation through such temporary benefits. In fact the effect of a mantra is delivered only when the essence of the mantra is known at an experiential level. Mere chanting without experiential understanding does not serve the ultimate purpose.

Seeker A: When I was in Varanasi, I saw some people reciting mantras. Out of curiosity, I also recited the "Om" mantra. To my surprise, my mind calmed down after some time. But after couple of hours, when I recited the mantra again, I didn't get the same result.

Sirshree: When you did it for the first time, your mind wasn't expecting its result. Hence, you got the result. However, when you did it for the second time, your mind already anticipated the result. Hence, the mind couldn't calm down due to anxiety and expectation.

Seeker A: Right. I was hoping for the same result.

Seeker B: What about teachers who claim to be gurus by teaching yoga or physical exercises? We see many such instructors and trainers, who help us work with our bodies. They make people workout in gyms or in yoga workshops and help them become physically fit and healthy. Many people consider such trainers as their gurus and follow them. I agree that physical fitness is important. Yoga has its own important place in the world in helping people become healthier at any age. But how can it be related to the truth?

Sirshree: Yoga is an ancient science which was initially conjoined with the truth. Unfortunately as the wheels of time turned, yoga remained limited to Asanas (postures) alone instead of being a bridge for union with the experience of the ultimate truth.

Seeker A: Some people learn yoga from India and practice it in other countries in the name of spirituality. People indeed get misled by them. While they do attain physical fitness, they remain bereft of the ultimate truth.

Sirshree: Then there are some who claim to be a guru by the number of followers they amass. If you want to meet them, you need to stand in long queues and pay for meeting them.

Seeker A: I have heard about such teachers. Their followers are told, "If you want an express appointment with them, you'll have to pay a premium. Only such people will attain salvation. Others will not." How can one buy salvation with money? Also, how can only specific followers attain salvation and not others?

Sirshree: One cannot buy salvation with money. In fact, money can never reduce or increase your sins. You can't buy piety with money. And definitely you can't attain salvation by simply seeing someone! Such practices only misguide people; they can never guide people towards the ultimate truth.

Seeker A: Right. I also know of some people, who claim to be gurus by being leaders of their communities or sects. Listening to their inspiring words, people do feel motivated and capable of achieving success in various ventures.

Sirshree: There are motivational trainers whose inspiring words can help in achieving worldly success. There are also leaders of communities who inspire people to promote the ideologies of their community. However, these words do not arise from the stillness of pure consciousness. Words arising from the plane of concepts and ideologies cannot serve the purpose of attaining the ultimate truth. This is because the truth is beyond all concepts, beyond ideologies, beyond the mind and intellect. So it becomes farfetched to imagine that one can attain the truth through the guidance of such motivational speakers.

There are also some, who claim to be gurus by inheritance or lineage. They take over from the previous guru of the sect or lineage. However, with the passage of time, the successors forget the real aim, the original vision, and the essence of what their predecessors lived for. Designation, authority, power and appreciation become more important. Thus, they remain mere title holders, occupying the position that has been passed onto them.

Seeker B: Yes. But thankfully this was not the case with Sikhism. Guru Nanak was their first guru, followed by a lineage of nine successors. After ten human gurus, the Sikh scripture known as the Guru Granth Sahib was regarded as the final and eternal guru.

Sirshree: Right! This arrangement was made so that the actual truth and its teachings are passed to further generations without any adulteration. Those who deeply care for genuine truth seekers make such arrangements so that seekers are not deprived of the actual truth.

Seeker B: I have also seen programmes on the religion-related TV channels where the masters keep singing devotional songs or *kirtans* or even dance. Their activities revolve around singing hymns and food offerings.

Seeker A: I have been to such congregations. But I found that the participants were mainly interested in the food that would be served after the rituals. No one was discussing about the truth there.

There are also many information providers who claim to be gurus in their own right. They can be teachers, life coaches or even online marketing, business or media coaches.

Sirshree: Some people wrongly consider them as their guru. This is why the word "guru" has lost its true meaning. They are merely providers of information. They impart knowledge about subjects related to the external world. The true guru makes you aware of your inner world and prepares you for the ultimate truth.

Seeker A: Right. I suppose they can rather be called "guides" or "experts" in certain fields of activity; they can't help us attain the ultimate truth.

Sirshree: There are some who claim to be gurus by solving your problems through some sacrificial ritual or a medallion. People approach them with their issues and they give them such solutions that have nothing to do with the truth.

Seeker A: I have seen some people approach priests for their problems. If they want wealth, the priest asks them to worship Goddess Lakshmi for a given number of Tuesdays. If they have lost their valuables, then the priest suggests them to worship Lord Hanuman for a given number of Saturdays. I feel sorry for these people when I see them blindly adhering to these rituals. They seem to have no clue what they are doing and why; they just blindly follow what's been told.

Seeker B: In Christianity, people confess their sins and seek forgiveness in the presence of priests. Confession boxes are placed in churches for this purpose.

In Hinduism, the river Ganges is considered sacred and is personified as the Goddess Ganga. She is worshiped by the Hindus who believe that bathing in the river causes remission of their sins and facilitates liberation from the cycle of life and death, and that the water of the Ganges is considered sacred.

Sirshree: When people can't easily do away with their feeling of guilt or regret, they find it difficult to live happily and peacefully, being in the present. They tend to live in the past and dwell in wrongdoings committed by them or others. Such rituals help them get relieved off their sins and negative feelings, and allow them to live life afresh.

Seeker A: It is difficult to lead a good life without seeking confession often. I have been visiting confession once a week if possible, once a month at the least as a ritual, even though I have no mortal sins to confess. So far I was doing it as a mechanical activity, but henceforth I will follow it with the right understanding.

Sirshree: In fact, you can seek forgiveness every day. At the end of the day, seek forgiveness from all those whom you may have hurt knowingly or unknowingly through your thoughts, feelings, speech or actions. This will help you live each day afresh without any burden of the past.

Seeker A: I will surely practice it.

Sirshree: There are some people who claim to be a guru by denouncing gurus and those who follow gurus. They logically convince you not to follow any other guru but believe in your own intellect. The intellect likes to hear such things. The intellect prefers to be the master. But the real Guru principle is beyond the body, mind and also the intellect.

If one has not known the truth, one will remain content with half-baked knowledge and may get stuck in the intellect forever. The highest use of the intellect is in realizing its own limitations. Truth is beyond logic. The highest use of reasoning is in realizing the limited confines of logic when it comes to experiencing the truth.

The intellect should be trained for subtler contemplation to a point where it realizes the futility of stuffing knowledge. True wisdom lies in becoming empty. Become an empty flute through which divine music can flow.

Seeker B: There are some scriptural experts who claim to be gurus by studying various religious scriptures like the Vedas, the Gita, the Gyaneshwari, or the Dasbodh, the Bible or the Quran and summarizing their essence for the common man.

Today people have got so much held up with their daily chores that they don't find enough time or even inclination to go through such scriptures. At such times, it really helps to listen to these people and get to know about the teachings from the ancient scriptures.

Sirshree: Yes, it's a great service rendered by them. However, when they earn a good name, fame and honor from their followers, they believe themselves to be spiritual gurus. Thereafter, they don't get ready to listen to the essential truth for themselves from anybody else. Many of these service providers, who do commentaries on the scriptures show off their knowledge, without realizing that it is bloating their own ego. Thus, their own journey to the truth is hampered.

Seeker A: So many people from the West believe that learning scriptures is spirituality. Hence, they learn ancient languages like Sanskrit.

Sirshree: Yes, that's the biggest loss for earnest seekers of truth. They learn scriptures from these people in the name of spirituality and remain deprived of the essential truth, which is beyond words.

The scriptures have been venerated as the truth. They speak about the truth; they can point to the truth; but they are not the truth. The truth expressed in the scriptures arose from the experience of the Self that realized masters revelled in. But these words have been taken literally by seekers of the truth. As a result, seekers have been misled in their attempt to compare and match their own experience with their interpretation of these words, instead of finding the original experience within themselves. The scriptures are a reflection of the direct experience of the truth. They serve as a mirror. But the mirror is not the truth.

Moreover, the mirror is tainted with dust. The reflection of the truth has been distorted through years of interpretation and commentaries, mostly by those who lacked the direct experience of the Self.

Seeker A: Can you please elaborate this with an example?

Sirshree: Consider the grand aphorism declared in the Upanishads – "Aham Brahmasmi". This declaration arose from the experience of the Self. This has been literally translated by many as "I am God", "I am that all-pervading reality". However, such translations cause the seeker to believe that he is the God personified. However, the truth is that a person can never be God. The deeper import of the aphorism can be stated as, "God is the I-AM". This may sound grammatically incorrect. And yet, it means that God is the "I-AMness", the sense of existence, the living presence within every body-mind. This is what Jesus states as, "I AM that I AM".

Further, when the Self experiences itself through a body-mind, it becomes evident that this experience is not confined to that individual body, but encompasses all beings and objects in the universe. The universal "I" experientially realizes that "All is God". The underlying oneness of everything is experienced.

Interpretations and translations that do not arise from this experience of the Self mislead the seeker away from this essential oneness.

It is only with true faith and devotion that one can let go of such bookish knowledge and abide in the truth. It is then the depth and grandeur of the truth becomes evident.

Seeker B: I am keen to gain the wisdom of the ultimate truth.

Sirshree: You cannot borrow the truth from outside; it cannot be obtained from outside. This is because it is already available within you. When a true guru points at the truth within you, it is by this grace that true wisdom awakens within you.

Truth is subjective experience, not objective knowledge. It cannot be known as you would the other topics of the world. You can only experience it by "being" it. And to "be" it, you need to empty yourself. You need to empty yourself of all that you have learned about the truth. You need to release all the beliefs and knowledge that you have gathered this far. This requires true faith and devotion, which can be awakened in the presence of a true guru.

The true guru is a complete guru. His teachings and instructions have a very deep impact as they directly arise from the experience of the Self; they arise from the very Source – the quintessence of truth.

When you come in contact with a true guru, you don't remain the same. You get completely transformed. Thereafter, you get guided from your heart. The presence of a true guru awakens the guru within you. You do not just realize the truth, but also get established in the experience of the truth. You become free from vices and blossom with virtues. You open up to your infinite potential. You start working for the purpose why you have taken this birth.

4
Grace is the Only Way

Seeker A: When we are surrounded by so many different types of gurus, it's possible to get easily misled by them. Finding a true guru in one's life is indeed a grace.

Sirshree: Despite so many misguiding factors, it is that rare providence that offers itself as an opportunity in the form of a true guru. This can happen only by grace. Thus, finding a true guru in itself is a cause for celebration, for your life has been blessed with its true purpose. In that sense, attaining a human birth is a grace in itself.

Seeker A: We are already born human. But we have not done anything for that.

Sirshree: That's why it can be considered a grace. Self-realization is possible only in humans. It's not possible in any other living being. Humans alone have been blessed with the potential of attaining infinite possibilities; no other creature.

Seeker A: I am feeling blessed to be born a human!

Sirshree: Despite being born human, not everyone attains Self-realization. Many get distracted by the lures of the material world and remain astray from the real goal. Hence, it's required to receive the second form of grace, wherein the thirst to attain the ultimate truth of life arises within oneself.

Seeker A: I would really want to attain the truth. But I don't know whether I have the genuine thirst that it takes.

Sirshree: If this grace has been bestowed, then right from childhood, such seekers are drawn within with questions like: Who really am I? Am I this body? If I am not the body, then who am I? How did all this begin? Is there something beyond this visible life? Is it possible to attain liberation in this very lifetime?

These questions can arise in different ways. Some people tend to imagine "nothingness." They imagine a scenario where there is nothing in the universe. In their imagination, they progressively omit everything, including their bodies, from the universe. They then try to imagine how it would feel like in this "nothingness." They stumble upon the fact that there has to be someone present to know that there is nothing. This "knower" is ever-present and cannot be eliminated.

There are others who get doubts when they look at themselves in the mirror. They start doubting, "Is this really me?"

Questions arose in the mind of the Buddha before enlightenment: What is the purpose of life? Am I here to merely grow old and die? Is sorrow the truth of life? These questions led to his quest for the ultimate truth.

Seeker A: I also often wonder what the purpose of my life is. I feel it's all so temporary. At the end of my life, I will have to leave behind whatever material possessions I have attained. Then why should I waste my priceless life in hankering after these fleeting pleasures? There has to be something more for which I am born instead of just living each day.

Sirshree: The mere fact that you have the thirst to know the purpose of your life indicates that the second grace has been bestowed on you.

Seeker B: I don't get such questions. And to be honest, I still have desires for material possessions and worldly success. Does that mean that I will be deprived of attaining the truth?

Sirshree: (laughs) No, you won't be deprived. When those who don't have the thirst for attaining the truth meet a true guru and instead of focusing on the external aspects of the guru such as his language, appearance, age, etc., focus only on his teachings, then the guru can awaken the thirst for the truth within them.

Then such a thirst turns into an intense prayer. In such a prayer, the seeker doesn't ask for materialistic or worldly things. Instead, one only asks for God or guru. One would pray: "O God, so far, I have asked for a lot of other things from You. But now You alone are my desire; nothing less than You will suffice."

Seeker B: I am really happy to know that I too can attain the truth. I will surely offer this prayer.

Sirshree: The third form of grace occurs when a true guru arrives in your life. Even when the thirst for attaining the truth has arisen, if a true guru doesn't arrive in your life, then you don't progress on your journey of the truth. Only a true guru knows from his own experience as to which seeker will get inspired by what action or thought, so as to progress towards the truth.

The knowledge of the truth is not new; it is ancient. What is needed is *real* knowledge which arises from the experience of Self, which is only possible with a true guru.

Seeker B: In today's hi-tech world, when so much knowledge is easily available on the internet, it's important to know which one is apt for our real growth. Otherwise we may fall victim to the fake gurus who either do not know the truth or know it only in words, without having ever experienced it.

Seeker A: What is the acid test for identifying a true guru?

Sirshree: The teachings of a true guru transform your life and bring happiness as opposed to the teachings of fake gurus. You experientially realize who you truly are. When the guru's teachings become part of your life, your life gets transformed in a true sense. Otherwise, many will perform miracles but if that doesn't help you experience the truth or bring real happiness in your life, then they are not true gurus. Hence, it's said that if a true guru has arrived in your life, then it is one of the greatest grace that has been bestowed on you. The light of grace guides you towards your highest good and brings unparalleled peace and fulfillment. Be in as much gratitude as you can for this.

Seeker B: Is it then enough to be with a true guru to attain Self-realization?

Sirshree: Just being with a guru is not enough. You also need to have unshakable faith in him. When you build firm faith and conviction in the guru, surrender unto him, then it can be said that the fourth form of grace has been bestowed on you.

Every seed has the potential of growing into a tree. But not all seeds grow to become trees. Similarly, only those disciples, who have unshaken faith on the guru and are nurtured with the light of grace, the water of faith, and the soil of understanding, reach the ultimate goal.

Seeker B: What exactly happens when one develops unshakable faith in the guru?

Sirshree: As one develops unshakable faith in the guru, one becomes eligible to receive the truth. The guru checks whether the disciple is ready to listen to the final truth, how prepared is he, does he have all the requisite qualities, is he ready to listen to the truth with an open mind, what is the possibility of the truth being revealed through him? When he finds the disciple eligible, then he imparts the final truth. Then the fifth form of grace is bestowed on the disciple.

Seeker A: Yes. I am realizing the importance of a true guru. One can't unfold his or her possibilities and progress in the journey of the truth unless he gets the right guru in his life.

Seeker B: But I am unable to understand what is meant by listening to the truth with an open mind?

Sirshree: When you listen to the truth in such a manner that it doesn't get adulterated by your preconceived notions and prior imaginations; neither is there any comparison or judgement, then it can be said that you are listening with an open mind. You listen to the truth as it is, where you become "the ear" itself, you become completely deceit-free and open. When this happens then it can be said that you have become eligible.

Seeker A: I am keen to know what exactly happens when the fifth form of grace occurs?

Sirshree: The fifth grace occurs when the One who bestows the grace and the one on whom the grace is being bestowed are no longer separate; their inherent oneness is revealed. There is a realization at the level of experience that Guru, God, Grace and the real-you are one.

If the first four kinds of grace have occurred, then the fifth grace is bound to happen. After the first four kinds of grace are bestowed, especially the fourth, then there is no further difficulty or uncertainty. This is because there is nothing that remains to be achieved. The veil of your beliefs, the curtain of false notions, need to be merely taken off. You are already there. The moment it is unveiled; the truth is revealed.

Seeker B: What do I need to do to obtain the guru's grace?

Sirshree: Although obtaining the guru's grace is not in your hands, it is important that you are available in the presence of the guru. The easiest way to do so is through devotional service *(seva)*. The easiest way to achieve success is to be with those who are already successful. So is it with Self-realization. Be in the company of those who are working towards it, who are ahead of you. Be in the presence of your guru. Be in service of your guru. As you do so, the guru observes you. Thus, you give him more opportunities to understand the nature of your body-mind. He may test you through various situations. How you respond shows how much faith you have on the guru.

In your service, the guru might question you. He will check whether the service you are giving is personalized or impersonal in intent. Thus he will guide you step by step.

Seeker A: I feel like our body is like a candle which has a wax and a thread. The guru is that radiant lamp in whose company the candle gets lit and realizes its full potential. Unless the experience of the Self is attained, how can our life ever be fulfilled?

Seeker B: Unless the experience of Self is attained, we wander in the endless pursuits of this world, bump onto numerous roadblocks in the dark. It's indeed a grace to get a true guru in our life. Unless we are in the vicinity of someone whose candle is already lit, how can our candle get lit?

Sirshree: The purpose behind every knock delivered by the guru, the intention behind the knowledge imparted by the guru, is to break your inherent patterns. It is with his grace alone that wisdom is born. It is only through the grace of the guru that the attainment of the final understanding becomes possible.

Attaining a true guru is God's grace;

Attaining God is the guru's grace;

Grace of the guru is the final grace;

Grace is the only way.

Seeker A: Earlier you had said that there is only one guru, which is the Consciousness within. Now we are discussing about an external guru. How are they related?

Sirshree: There is only one guru, the Consciousness within, the Self. The Self wants to experience itself through you. However, the contrast mind which is the comparing and judging mind, has shrouded the experience of the Self. Due to the confusion in the body-mind mechanism, the Self is not able to experience its nature directly. To work around this, the Self imparts understanding and clears the confusion by means of an external body of the guru, where the Self has already realized itself.

Seeker A: I am still not clear. Can you please clarify it further?

Sirshree: Let's imagine that there is a mike inside you. Suppose that the Universal Consciousness, the Self, wants to speak through that mike. However, the mike is covered with thick layers of cloth due to which you are unable to hear the voice directly. Therefore, Consciousness speaks to you through an external body-mind mechanism, where the layers of cloth (the contrast mind) have already disappeared. Consciousness is always speaking to you, but you are unable to hear it. This is why an external guru is required.

In and through the various situations in your life, you are being taught vital life lessons. In that sense, life itself is the guru. However, when you get entangled in various situations and are unable to decode the life lessons hidden in them, then the guru essence manifests through an external form to explicitly convey those lessons to you.

There is only one guru – the Self. In fact, it is the Self that creates the desire for liberation, it is the Self that bestows the light of grace in the form of the guru's body, it is the Self that imparts the final understanding through the guru's body. It is through the grace of the Self that the quest ends in its own attainment. Guru, God, Grace and the real-you are one.

Saint Kabir once said, "In front of me stand both – Guru and God. Before whom do I prostrate first? I will prostrate before my guru, because it is by my guru's grace that I am able to see

God (realize the Self or the truth)."

Seeker B: Can I attend to more than one guru at the same time?

Sirshree: You may seek guidance from more than one guru, but this has an inherent risk. You may end up making your "own mind" the guru and go by its judgments. The very mind that is the obstacle to the truth. It is only when the judging mind drops that the Self shines. The judging mind will choose to follow whatever appeals to it. Thus, following more than one guru is akin to making "the mind" the guru. In the process, the mind becomes stronger and more obstinate.

Can you ask a thief the best way to catch him? No! He is bound to misguide you, so as to avoid being caught. So it is with the mind. A strong mind cannot annihilate itself. You need guidance from one who leads you beyond the mind; who leads your mind to surrender to the ultimate truth in devotion.

5
The Need and Urgency for Self-Realization

Seeker B: I was speaking with my friends about the ultimate purpose of life. However, my friends were raising doubts regarding this. I couldn't get satisfactory answers to put their doubts to rest. They were saying: Life can go on even without realizing the Self. There are so many people who have not realized the Self and yet are able to lead a good life.

Sirshree: Who is in a better position to determine the merits of having a computer at home: the person who has experiential knowledge of the computer, or the one who doesn't?

Seeker B: Definitely, the one who possesses the knowledge and experience of using a computer can alone talk about whether it is needed or not, whether it is beneficial or not.

Sirshree: When the computer was invented, most people were against the spread of automation. They feared that people would lose their jobs due to the onset of computing automation. Initially, when various institutions, banks and government offices were computerized, many people protested against such initiatives. Only those who later used the computer could talk about its necessity.

Drawing parallels from this example, who do you think is in the best position to determine whether Self-realization is required or not?

Seeker A: The one who has attained Self-realization alone can comment on whether it is essential or not and its impact on our lives.

Sirshree: That's right! It may seem logical that one can lead a good life without attaining Self-realization. However, if everyone suffers from a disease, then they do not sense it as a disease. Therefore, they do not feel the need to get admitted in the hospital. One who is cured from the disease alone can justify the need of a hospital.

Seeker B: My friends feel it's so arduous to undertake this journey. If life can be so easy even without it, why should we take it up?

Sirshree: Before concluding whether it is difficult, they need to experience it. Until you experience the Self, you have no right to judge or conclude about it. People who are blinded by ignorance unknowingly try to mislead others.

It is only after you climb to the hilltop that you can determine whether it is difficult to climb the hill. If you have never been to the hilltop, then how can you even talk about how it is at the summit?

He who has attained Self-realization alone can state whether it is easy or difficult to reach that state. If one is unaware of the experience of the Self, then how can one determine the ease or difficulty of attaining that state?

Seeker A: Very true!

Sirshree: When one questions the need to attain Self-realization, he never doubts his own question. He commits this grave mistake out of ego. He never questions his own doubts. He makes his own judgements and draws conclusions. But he never doubts that his conclusions could be wrong. He questions, but never doubts the basis of his own questions. He never contemplates on his questions, nor does he try to find the answers by himself.

Actually as one begins to understand the truth, one gradually understands that he does not even know how to ask the right questions. After the guru enters a seeker's life, it has been found that all the questions of the seeker dissolve. This happens because the state of Self-realization is already attained by the body-mind of the guru. Hence, the guru is able to guide the seeker towards Self-realization, where everything is clearly seen and no questions remain.

A person disagrees to the existence of life after death. Another person says that he believes in life after death. But they need to be questioned whether their conclusions are based on sound research, or on deep contemplation? Have they put in any efforts to seek the truth? If they haven't, then how can they blindly assert their belief or the lack of it?

Seeker A: What do we do then?

Sirshree: You need to go beyond both, trust and distrust. You ought to first listen to something, enquire and reflect on it. The guru instructs you to contemplate deeply on any topic before raising questions on it. Then alone do you have the right to ask questions. Do not ask questions merely for the sake of it. First consider how much you have contemplated on it. Before asking anything, first doubt the mind – with what authority and basis is the mind questioning? To what extent have you researched on the topic?

Seeker B: Whenever I share with my uncle about seeking the truth, he always preaches, "This is your time to excel in the world. Practice spirituality after you are 50 years. You do not need to indulge in it now."

Sirshree: Some people preach with such confidence! But they lack right knowledge. They need to sincerely reflect whether this knowledge needs to be attained after 50 years of age or as early as possible. Had they reflected on it, tried to seek the truth and understood it, they would have agreed to the urgency of attaining this knowledge as early in life as possible. If you doubt your own doubts and questions, then alone can you attain the truth. Without contemplation, the search for truth stops.

Seeker B: But how does the guru help at this juncture?

Sirshree: After the guru enters your life, he imparts you the eye of wisdom. You then realize what liberation is and whether it is essential to attain it. With the light of grace, you realize that true spirituality is common sense. The guru then guides you along the path. Otherwise, the seeker gets entangled in questions, doubts and judgements. He never doubts his own questions and remains stuck in them. He always feels that nobody is able to answer his questions. He feels superior about the fact that he has so many "super" questions and none of them are answered.

Seeker B: When is the guru needed the most in the spiritual journey? Is it in the beginning, in the middle, or towards the end?

Sirshree: The guru is required most towards the end. In the beginning, the desire to attain the truth has to increase. Your desire to attain the truth can be aroused even by reading a relevant book. You listen to truth discourses and your desire intensifies. At least, a beginning is made. There are many who begin, but their journey does not progress.

Towards the middle, this desire increases. You have begun to understand. You have begun to receive wisdom that brings about transformation.

Towards the end, the disciple has understood the truth intellectually. However, just because he knows it intellectually, he might assume himself as being Self-realized and may now be unwilling to journey further. He may feel, "I know everything. I don't need to know anything beyond this." This state is akin to that of an elephant that has passed through the doorway, but its tail is stuck at the door. It is at this juncture that the guru is needed the most. If you have faith on the guru, you will listen to him and attain the experience of truth.

Here "towards the end" denotes the end of the spiritual quest and not the end of life. There is also a risk that the disciple may become content too soon. He is yet to reach the summit, but he may conclude that he has done so, when he is seated on a plateau. The guru is required there to give him a final push. The guru is needed at all times, but most towards the end.

Seeker B: I realize the importance of a guru now. I also understand that once a true guru enters our life, we need to be fully receptive to him, listen to the truth, contemplate on his teachings and abide by his instructions.

Sirshree: You are doing this for your own benefit. This will help awaken *Viveka* – the power of truth-discrimination within you. You will be able to discriminate between the truth and untruth. When you consistently use this power of truth-discrimination, you will be propelled towards the ultimate goal.

Seeker A: This is a grace for those who have a true guru in their lives. But what about those who have not been blessed with a true guru in their lives? How can they be guided at each and every step in their journey of life?

Sirshree: There is only one guru, the Consciousness within, the Self. It guides you through an external body. If no such external guru has come into your life, you can seek guidance within yourself from Consciousness. You need to follow some steps for that.

- Step 1: Ask – The first and the foremost step is ask for guidance. When you pray, you seek guidance from Consciousness. Pray every day for a true guru.

- Step 2: Aware – After having prayed, remain aware to receive the results of your prayer. Be on the lookout: Now that the answer to my prayer is going to arrive, let me see from where it comes. Whoever meets you can bring the answer to your prayer. You should be alert and receptive for that answer. It is crucial to maintain such awareness;

otherwise people often forget after offering a prayer. After praying, wherever you go, try to catch the indications being presented to you. The answer will definitely come to you, some way or the other.

- Step 3: Act – After having prayed and being aware, you will receive the answer. You then have to act on the answer. If you have received the answer in the form of a message, then begin to act on it, do not keep waiting. For example, someone tells you that a spiritual discourse will be held on a particular day on a particular topic. On getting this message, if you do not attend it, it means that even after getting the answer to your prayer, you were not able to perceive it. Therefore, get into action as soon as you get an indication. Do not delay.

- Step 4: Analyze – After having received the message and acted on it, analyze it. Reflect upon it: What was the message? How did I decode it? Have I acted correctly or not? What was its result? In this way, you would be able to analyze your actions.

Seeker A: It's good to know about these four steps. If we miss any of these, then we may easily lose our way.

6
Transcending the Body-Mind Temperaments

Seeker A: I always wonder if during the war of Mahabharata, Lord Krishna had been approached by Duryodhana instead of Arjuna, would he have guided him the same way as he guided Arjuna?

Sirshree: No. Lord Krishna would have guided him differently. He would have delivered a completely different Gita to him, considering the nature of his body-mind. In fact, his words would have been entirely different from what was used for Arjuna.

Seeker B: But Gita is a doctrine of the universal truth. It's message is universal. Then how can it change from one person to another?

Sirshree: While the truth is the same, how it applies to each body-mind can vary. This is because each body-mind is different. Take a simple example: Some people feel sleepy after a night shower, whereas some feel fresh and wide awake.

At a deeper level, each one has a different set of beliefs. Some believe in idol worship, whereas some believe in the formless God. Some believe in destiny, whereas some believe in *karma*. Some highly regard selfless service, whereas some treat chanting and remembrance of God as everything. Some find spirituality in having talismans and smearing ash on their foreheads while some find it in singings hymns. Some are receptive to guidance through visuals, some through words whereas some are receptive through feelings. Thus, every body-mind is different and needs different guidance as per its nature and temperament. A true guru understands this and guides each one accordingly.

Therefore, the Gita that was recited for Arjuna would have changed for Duryodhana or Shakuni. While Arjuna is motivated to take up arms to wage the war of righteousness, Duryodhana would have been incited to lay down his arms and surrender to what is righteous, considering his nature, temperament, and position in the overall scheme of things.

Seeker A: What are these temperaments that vary from one person to the other? Can you please elaborate?

Sirshree: There are three primary temperaments that govern the human body-mind mechanism. They are *Sattva, Rajas* and *Tamas*. These three *gunas* (qualities, attributes) determine the disposition of the human body-mind.

Tamas is the tendency of inertia or passivity. *Rajas* is the tendency of movement or activity. *Sattva* is the tendency of equanimity or balance. The proportion of these three temperaments within the human body-mind shapes its overall behavior. This is why you find people prone to a variety of dispositions.

Seeker B: I have heard about them. People with *tamas* tend to prefer stale or preserved food; they somehow don't like fresh and wholesome food. They are laid-back and find solace in pleasures that stimulate their senses. People with *rajas* typically prefer hot and spicy food, which they eat quickly. *Sattva*-predominant people eat to live; they don't live to eat. They are sensitive to the effects of food on the body and mind. They always eat a well-balanced and optimum quantity of food.

Sirshree: Yes, but these temperaments are not just limited to physical existence. The play of these temperaments is subtle and unseen. It manifests at all levels of human existence – physical, mental, intellectual and occupational.

Tamas is characterized by lethargy, inertia, passivity, ignorance, greed and attachment to lowly desires. A *tamasic* mind indulges in base thoughts and negative emotions like hatred, anger and ill-will. A *tamasic* intellect is dull and rigid.

A *tamasic* body is prone to lethargy. If they find that something can be done in sleeping position instead of a sitting, they prefer the sleeping position. If something can be done in a sitting position instead of standing, they prefer to sit. And if a vehicle can transport them from one place to another without having to walk, they prefer that option. "Rest" is their topmost priority in any activity they do.

Seeker B: People with *tamas* also find it difficult to get up early.

Sirshree: Right. A *tamasic* person tends to be listless in his ways and shy away from action and efforts. He also has the tendency to be deceitful.

Rajas is the quality that fuels activity. It serves as an engine for active and productive life. However, when this engine goes into overdrive, the result is hyperactivity. *Rajasic* people tend to be extremely hyperactive and energetic. They are always focused on what they should do next. They are highly ambitious, whether or not they have the qualities to achieve them. They are rarely satisfied with whatever they have and constantly seek new sensations and variety in life. They are always running around, worrying about things and always engaging in some sort of action – whether beneficial or otherwise.

They find it difficult to relax and stay still, both physically and mentally. Even if they are forced to sit at one place, they keep moving around. Such people find it difficult to even power themselves down and sleep at night. They are high on action even then.

Seeker A: They seem to be the other extreme of *tamasic* people. How about *Sattva?*

Sirshree: *Sattva* is the quality of equanimity and balance. It is the subtlest and most intangible of the three qualities. *Sattva* expresses as composure, level-headedness, purity and virtuousness.

Sattvic people do not over-indulge in any one thing. They tread the middle path of balance between work and rest. They make optimum use of sleep, activity and rest.

Seeker B: This middle path seems interesting. Can you please elaborate it further?

Sirshree: Let's understand it with the way the human heart functions. The heart beats around 72 times a minute on average, but also relaxes 72 times a minute. Due to this balance between work and rest, it can ceaselessly function for a very long time, sometimes for even more than hundred years. *Sattva*-predominant people are privy to this secret and emulate this example of the heart. They rest before they get tired and resume activity before lethargy sets in.

Seeker B: This is truly a classic example of the middle path!

Seeker A: If these *gunas* are so different from one another, how does the guru guide such seekers?

Sirshree: The guru exactly knows which things accelerate the seeker in their spiritual journey and guides them accordingly. For a *tamasic* seeker, the guru acts like a whip. He forces him to get into action. For a *rajasic* seeker, the guru acts like a comma in a sentence. He motivates them to take a pause and maintain balance between activities. He guides them to relax between two activities. For a *sattvic* seeker with equanimity, the guru acts like a mirror to bring the seeker's ego into light.

Let's understand this with the help of an example:

Children have the habit of sucking their thumbs. Their mothers know very well how to break this habit of theirs. If the child is *sattvic,* his mother will have to pull his thumb out of his mouth just a couple of times, and that will be enough to break his habit.

If that doesn't do the trick, she applies some bitter juice to the child's thumb, like that of a bitter gourd. The child tastes the bitter juice and gives up the habit.

If the child is *tamasic,* the mother has to resort to a harsher method. She applies red chili powder to the thumb to jolt the child out of the habit.

In the above example, the mother's actions might appear cruel and harsh, but she knows how important it is for the child to get out of the habit. Some mother, out of ignorance or out of blind love for her child, might even apply sugar syrup to the child's thumb, thereby worsening the habit, instead of breaking it. This particular example points to those fraudulent gurus who, instead of thwarting the disciple's misbeliefs, make them even stronger by misguiding them. However, a true guru knows how essential it is to free the disciple from false beliefs, assumptions and imaginations, even if that causes the disciple some temporary discomfort.

Seeker A: One of my friends is highly *rajasic* in nature. He is constantly engaged in some sort of activity or the other. I wonder how the guru can motivate such seekers to take a pause in between?

Sirshree: (laughs) Understand this with the help of a story:

A person once went to his guru and narrated his woes, "I have so many responsibilities towards my family and at the workplace that I don't get even a second for myself. I have to find my son a good job, take care of my ill wife and find a suitor for my daughter…" And he went on with his never ending list of problems, concerns and worries.

The guru heard him out very attentively and patiently. When the man was done with his speech, the guru summoned another disciple and asked him to lock up the man in another room. At first, the man was shocked and angry. He had come in anticipation of some relief for his problems. He didn't expect such a response from the guru. He kept banging the door from inside, deploring this action of the guru and pleading to be let out so that he could get back to his family and his duties, but the guru didn't pay heed to him.

After a month, when he was let out, he rushed back home. He was shocked to see that his son had found a job and his wife's health had improved quite a bit too. Everything happened smoothly and effortlessly. He realized what the guru wanted to teach him in this incident. The guru acted as a break, a comma for him.

Seeker A: This is an eye-opener! What the person wanted happened without his intervention. This is such an illogical solution.

Seeker B: I believe when *tamasic* people are forced into action or *rajasic* people are asked to take a pause, they actually become *sattvic*.

Sirshree: That's right. Before they are put on the path to Self-realization, they first need to become *sattvic*. This will help them change their perception and attitude towards life.

Let's understand how the guru brings about this change with the help of a story:

A king approached his guru with a problem, "O revered guru! An intense thirst has arisen within me to relinquish my kingdom and dedicate my remaining life in spiritual pursuit. But, I am not getting a suitable heir. My son is too young to shoulder this responsibility. What do I do?"

The guru replied, "Why don't you hand over your kingdom to me? Do you hope to find anyone more deserving and capable than me?"

The king was exhilarated at this proposition. He replied, "There can be no one better than you to run my kingdom. I hand over to you the responsiblity of this kingdom from this very moment!"

"What do you plan to do now?" asked the guru.

The king pondered over it for a few moments and replied, "I shall take some money from the kingdom's treasury, just enough to lead the rest of my life."

"You are forgetting that you just handed over your kingdom to me," replied the guru, "which means the treasury also belongs to me, and I will not permit you to take any money from it!"

A little disconcerted, the king was lost in thought. After some time, he replied, "Very well then, I will manage to find odd-jobs that will pay me enough to get by."

Closely assessing the king's state of mind, the guru asked, "In case you are looking for a job, I have a vacancy that you might consider. Would you be interested?"

A little relieved, the king replied, "Yes of course! I am willing to do any job."

"The vacancy I have is that of a king," replied the guru with a serious tone, "I want you to take up the job of being the king of this kingdom and draw a salary from the treasury every month in return for your services."

A year later, the guru visited the king and found that he was happily performing all his kingly duties and at the same time was also able to devote time to spirituality – something he was willing to give up his kingdom for!

So, what had changed for the king? Nothing at all! It was the same king, the same kingdom and the same duties. What changed was his perception and attitude towards life. He was rid of the burden of his responsibilities, even while he continued to perform his duties. This is what the guru does. He changes your paradigm, your perspective and attitude towards life!

Seeker B: This is really insightful! I would love to become *sattvic*. What do I need to do?

Sirshree: Everyone would love to become *sattvic* after knowing its virtues. It's very much in our power to increase the temperament we want. All the three *gunas* are present in everyone in different proportions. It's not that *sattva* is totally absent in *tamas* or *rajas* predominant people. Some amount of *sattva* is alive even in the most *tamasic* or *rajasic* people. It's just that it has been muted and has become dormant because they have constantly ignored it in favor of *tamas* or *rajas*.

The secret to develop *sattva* is to program your subconscious mind with habits that promote *sattva*. You can begin with your eating habits. An oft-repeated saying is that you are what you eat. Program your mind to enjoy easily digestible, nutritious and energizing food. Avoid heavy, fatty, spicy, sugary, processed and preserved food.

When you begin with reforming the habits of your body, your mind too will follow suit. When we begin from the bottom and move upwards, we automatically receive cues from nature regarding what to do next. Act upon the cues and develop *sattvic* habits. Soon enough, you will find yourself enjoying a *sattvic* lifestyle.

However, here's a word of caution: Being *sattvic* is not the ultimate goal of life. There are dangers of remaining stuck with the *sattvic* way of life without seeking to go beyond it.

Seeker B: I was of the opinion that equanimity can help in stilling the mind and being in the experience of Self. How could being *sattvic* be dangerous?

Sirshree: Many people who take to spirituality consider the progression to the *sattvic* way of life as the final goal. There are dangers inherent in resting on the plateau of *sattva*, without going beyond it.

The biggest danger is the probability of backsliding into *tamas*. If *sattvic* people are unaware that there is something beyond *sattva*, they can become complacent, egoistic and arrogant.

"I know it all" is a very dangerous belief. People who have the arrogance of "I know it all" can get trapped in the mire of *sattva*. They tend to be lost in intellectual delights.

It is like someone who is prescribed a pill by the doctor to cure his disease. But instead of curing himself by consuming the pill, he uses it like an incense stick to show off its fragrance to others around him.

Sattvic people can fall into the trap of flaunting the knowledge that they gain from the guru, instead of digesting it to transform themselves. Such knowledge is mere information, not true wisdom. True progress happens only when one becomes empty off all notions and lives like an empty flute, through which divine music can be played.

Sattvic people get into selfless service. However, they tend to take credit for performing altruistic deeds for the wellbeing of society. So, even if they have moved away from negative karma, they have got attached to positive karma. It's like instead of iron handcuffs, they are bound to golden handcuffs. True wisdom lies in surrendering all deeds to the Self. However, they revel in a sense of self-pride for being the doer of noble deeds.

Sattva-predominant people need to progress, by transcending both – negative and positive *karma*.

It can be considered unfortunate for someone who has come near the ultimate state to then backslide due to complacency or arrogance. It would be sad because this person had overcome *tamas* and *rajas* and had the momentum to transcend the *gunas*.

Seeker A: What is the state beyond *sattva?*

Sirshree: To be able to understand the state beyond *sattva,* you need to first understand that these *gunas* are temperaments of your body, mind and intellect; they are not *your* qualities. You are not your body, mind or intellect. Your essential nature is Consciousness, the Self. The Self presides over the body, mind and intellect. You are not a pawn in the hands of your *gunas*; you are the master of your *gunas*. It is you who needs to take control of them and not the other way round.

The state that is beyond the three *gunas* is known as the *Gunateet* state, pure Consciousness – the state that transcends these temperaments of your body-mind mechanism. In this state of conscious presence, you can make use of the three *gunas* as and when you require them for Self-expression at your discretion, without being susceptible to their influence.

Seeker A: Can you please further explain the *Gunateet* state?

Sirshree: The *gunateet* state is a state of Self-stabilization, where one is established in the experience of the Self. You don't need external motivation to lead life in this manner. If the need is to get up and do something, you simply activate the *rajas guna* and start doing it. At bedtime, you make use of *tamas* to get into deep sleep. While meditating, you make controlled use of *tamas* and *sattva* to enter into deep state of stillness. When some activity needs to be done, you make use of *rajas* and perform the activity. Thus, for everything that you need to do, you have your *gunas* at your disposal.

You are aware that you are employing the *gunas* for the divine purpose of your body-mind; hence you don't get attached to them. You experience yourself as the detached witnesser of all activity. You recognize that you are not defined by your *gunas*. You clearly see your *gunas* as mere tools. You choose your tools; the tools don't choose you. You make a wise decision every time because you are not swayed by your temperaments. This is true Self-mastery.

Seeker B: Will I be distanced from the world, if I am in the *gunateet* state?

Sirshree: No. The *gunateet* state doesn't distance you from the world. You take part in every activity that you need to. Inspired actions arise from the Self and express through your body-mind. You connect and transact with the world, but you are not attached to it. You have a top-view of things. You express divine love for people; not "personalized" love that is related to the body and mind. Every activity becomes a means of Self-expression instead of fueling the ego.

Seeker A: I can see that I am often tied down by the grip of *tamas*. I escape action and prefer to follow the path of least resistance. I can strive to raise myself to a *sattvic* life. But is it ever possible for me to attain such an exalted state that you've described?

Sirshree: It is possible to attain this state, because it's already available within you. If it had to be acquired from elsewhere, then it wouldn't have been possible. You need to raise your level of consciousness by listening to the truth, through service unto the truth, through devotion of the truth.

Begin by raising your awareness to spot the play of the temperaments. Notice when *tamas* dominates your choices. Observe where *rajas* takes you away from the state of relaxed alertness. Be vigilant about how the ego bloats about *sattvic* qualities. With heightened awareness, you will be able to spot when *tamas, rajas* and *sattva* are at work in your body-mind.

For example, consider the situation when you decide to sit in meditation. If you are *sattva*-predominant, you will immediately sit in meditation. Spot the rise of *tamas* or *rajas* here. If you feel like resting or procrastinating, *tamas* is at work. If you feel like watching your favorite TV show or doing some work or activity, *rajas* is at work. Watch the play of temperaments unrelentingly, while abiding in the experience of conscious presence.

You need to raise your awareness so that you not only move from *tamas* to *sattva*, but also transcend sattva into the stateless state of the Self.

7
Role of the Guru

Seeker A: Can you please explain in more detail, how the guru functions in our life?

Sirshree: Yes. How would you feel looking at a winged bird that doesn't know how to fly?

Seeker A: I will feel pity for it. Despite having the potential to fly, it's unable to. It can't experience the joy of flying.

Sirshree: And how would you feel if the bird takes flight looking at some other bird flying in the sky?

Seeker A: I will thank the other bird, due to which this bird could realize its ability to fly.

Sirshree: So, you've got the answer to your question! That's how the guru functions. The guru functions like the other bird. The mere presence of the guru is an inspiration for others. Let's understand it with a riddle, which is like a Zen koan.

Imagine a cupboard that can lock its own doors by itself. One day the cupboard locks itself up with the key to the cupboard kept inside. There is no spare key to the lock and the single key that can open it, lies inside the locked cupboard. How can the cupboard be opened now?

Seeker B: Logically it seems impossible to open it without a key.

Sirshree: Drawing a parallel to the above example, if one were to think illogically, the solution would be to keep an open cupboard next to the locked cupboard. Being in the presence of an open cupboard, the locked cupboard will open itself.

The open cupboard is a metaphor of the guru. Just the presence of the enlightened guru in your life can open up innumerable doors within your mind, that lead to your own upliftment and stabilization in the Self. The guru is not only conscious of his true Self, he is stabilized in that experience. In that sense, his mere presence is a great help for mankind.

Seeker A: So far, I have regarded helping someone physically as a kind of service. I never thought that one's mere presence can also become a service. It's a great insight.

Sirshree: You can't help others until you are free from all help.

Seeker A: I could never think of helping others without anticipating help from them in return. I can't fathom there could be anyone who can help others without expecting anything in return.

Sirshree: The guru is an exception to this as he has risen above the need of any help and is stabilized in the experience of the Self. His presence alone helps to open up infinite possibilities of everyone. He is like an ocean in whose presence waves attain their fullest potential and dissolve. The give and take happens between waves but the ocean always remains a detached source. The waves could falter in their expression, but the ocean can never, as it is the substratum for all waves.

If we look at others' behavior and react, we may falter someday. But if we take inspiration from the guru, we will only reach the pinnacle of expression. Thus, the guru becomes a solid foundation of faith for the disciples which makes them believe that they too can attain stabilization in the Self in this very lifetime. They too can soar high in the sky.

Seeker B: I have read in some ancient Sanskrit scriptures, *"Gurur Brahma Gurur Vishnu Gurur Devo Maheshvara. Gurur Saakshaat ParaBrahma Tasmai Shree Guruve Namah."*

Sirshree: Such verses sing praises of the guru. The guru is in essence the embodiment of divine wisdom. He is the link between us and god. It may not be very easy for us to interact with god directly, but the guru serves as the channel through which we can connect with god.

God is formless. God is not a tangible existence. It may be difficult for most of us to perceive something that is devoid of form. The Guru principle is essentially the formless aspect of God. This Guru principle expresses itself through a human form where stabilization in the Self has happened. It is important to note that the guru does not seek the disciple's reverence for his own sake, as he is beyond it. However, reverence for this human form of the guru can make us receptive, thereby helping us take a peek into the formless essence of everything, called "God". In that sense, the guru serves as a bridge between us and god. Therefore, such verses regard the guru so highly. They treat the

Guru principle at par with god and the Guru's physical form as the embodiment of wisdom that leads one to God.

Seeker B: Each of us has a variety of beliefs, assumptions and imaginations. Then how does the guru help us become free from them?

Sirshree: The guru decides the method based on the nature of your body-mind mechanism. He also assesses how much faith and trust you have on him, how deeply rooted your beliefs are. At the outset itself, he asks for 100% trust from you.

Seeker A: I feel as if the guru would be doing some painful operation on me.

Sirshree: While you tread the path to the final truth, sometimes the guru needs to adopt difficult ways, which may make you feel that you are being deliberately put to task by him. But never doubt the guru's benevolent intention. Always have faith that the ultimate intention of the guru would always be to free you from all your bondages and patterns. Otherwise, with distrust, even the highest wisdom will fail to bring about the effect you seek in your life. It would be tantamount to not having the wisdom at all!

There is no cowardice in communicating your flaws to your guru and understanding how to fix them. It is in fact a wise and honest choice. If you don't trust the guru, who else will you?

Seeker A: Can you please elaborate more?

Sirshree: (laughs) Okay. Let us understand this with the help of a story:

A Zen master would raise his index finger upright when he used to preach. He would say, "I am not the body. I am that one universal presence that transcends both joy and sorrow."

In his ashram, a boy attendant used to serve tea to everyone. He used to imitate the master to the merriment of the other disciples. One day, while the master was away, the little boy started mimicking him before his disciples. He raised his index finger, just like the master would, and parroted the master's words.

Just as he was saying this, the master came in from behind and cut his index finger with a sharp knife. The two events occurred simultaneously – the boy was saying "I am *not* the body" and the master chopped off his finger.

The master said to the boy, "If you are *not* the body, then you're not the one who just lost a finger either!"

The moment the master's words fell upon the boy's ears, the ultimate truth dawned upon him. In a split second, he had understood the truth by experiencing his true Self beyond his body! He experientially realized that he was not the body.

Seeker A: That's a great story. An act that looked cruel and gruesome outwardly, turned out to be the reason for the boy's Self-realization.

Sirshree: This story depicts the importance of the guru. He attacks the mass belief – I am the body. This is the biggest, the most widespread and deeply rooted belief in each and every one. Had it been a belief specific to few individuals, they would have easily come out of it. But when everyone has the same belief, the whole world lives by this belief, then it becomes impossible to emerge out of it, without the grace of the guru.

The guru throws light on this profound belief, making you aware of it. He leads you to experience your true nature. When you experientially realize that you are not the body, that you are the Self, then you break free from this belief. It then becomes easy to break free from the wrong habits and tendencies. This is because it becomes clear to you that these habits are of the body and the mind; and you are neither the body, nor the mind.

Seeker B: Do you mean to say that this one-time realization is enough for us to break free from this belief? We don't forget it again.

Sirshree: No. After experientially realizing that you are the Self, if you have not got free from your wrong habits and inherent tendencies, they force you go back to an unconscious way of life. You then forget your true nature and continue to believe yourself to be the body. You get trapped in karmic bondage as a result.

The guru imparts you the understanding: Who is the doer? Who is enacting all the activities of this world? How does the mind step in and try to claim doer-ship of everything? How does the vacillating mind label every situation and get trapped in the web of its own thoughts?

As you reflect over it in and through each and every situation of your life, gradually you break free from these tendencies and wrong habits. You get liberated from their vicious cycle and are propelled towards the ultimate goal of life.

Sirshree: The guru delivers the final blow upon you.

Consider a bird that has been locked up in a cage for a long time – such a long time that it doesn't even remember how it it is like to be free. Even if you were to open the door of the cage to set the bird free, it still wouldn't leave. If you try to pull it out of the cage, it holds on to the bars of the cage. What's necessary here is a jerk to loosen its grip on the bars and prod it to take flight in the open sky.

Seeker B: What are you pointing at? What kind of cage are you referring to here?

Sirshree: It's the cage of the words of wisdom. A disciple might intellectually understand each and every word coming from the guru; he would also value those words the most, but would lack the experiential knowing of the same. The guru knows that the role of his words is just like the stick of an ice-cream candy. After you have enjoyed the candy, you throw the stick away. You don't save it as a souvenir. Likewise, the guru's words are important up to a certain state. Thereafter, when you begin to grasp the experiential essence of those words, the words need to be discarded, so as to attain a state of inner stillness and eternal silence.

If you are stuck in those words, then the guru delivers a final bolt. Just like you use an external thorn to remove a thorn stuck in your feet, the guru uses his words like a thorn to set you free from the cage of words.

Seeker A: After all, what is the kind of state that the guru wants us to attain?

Sirshree: The guru is stabilized in the state of *nothingness* and wants you to stabilize in the same state. This is the state of your true being. Attaining such a state and stabilizing in it is the ultimate goal of life. When you stabilize in that state, you experientially understand, "God alone is there. There is nothing except God." In that sense, the guru wants the disciple to become like himself. Exactly like himself – and nothing less.

Seeker B: I have read about the state of nothingness in books but have never experienced it. How can the guru help me attain this state at the experiential level?

Sirshree: Let's understand it through a story of a parrot:

Once upon a time, there was an unusual *talking* parrot, who had been locked up in a cage for a long time. One fine day, he came to know that his owner was going on a pilgrimage to meet up with his guru. He requested his owner, "Please also convey my salutations and my message to your guru. Tell him that I have been caged up for so many years now. On your return, please tell me what he replies."

The owner conveyed the parrot's message to the guru. Upon hearing the message, the guru fell silent. He closed his eyes and went into a deep meditative state. When the owner returned home, he recounted his experience to the parrot.

Hearing this, the parrot abruptly closed his eyes and fell down from the bar on which it was perched. Surprised by the parrot's behavior, the owner presumed that the parrot must have got deeply hurt with the guru's silent response and died. He opened the cage door to get the dead parrot out. As soon as he did that, the parrot flew away and sat on a tree's branch close by.

The shocked and angry owner cried out, "You cheated me! You

acted out to be dead but you are still alive."

The parrot replied, "I just followed your guru's advice and I am free today!"

So, what was the message conveyed by the guru?

Seeker B: The message was to get into meditation and set yourself free from the state of bondage. The parrot decoded this simple, straightforward message and just followed what the guru did to set himself free.

Sirshree: That's right! The guru delivers only one message: Take flight. Get into the state of deep meditation while you are alive. Die while you are still alive. Become what I have become. Become the universal "I".

Seeker A: I understand that by attaining the state of the guru, we will attain our ultimate goal of life. Is that the only reason why the guru wants us to be like him?

Sirshree: A true guru teaches us that we can't realize who we truly are by looking at others. However, we should become the one looking at whom others should realize their true nature. When you attain Self-realization, you become an inspiration for others to attain the same. You open up the prospect of attainment of Self-realization for everyone. By looking at you, others will set out on a journey to realize their true nature. Thus, the guru makes his disciples exactly like him, no less.

Seeker B: This is truly illogical! I would have never fathomed this. After all, how does the guru make this happen?

Sirshree: The mind is bound to get confused after hearing this. Just as the mind has preconceived notions and imaginations about god, so does it hold ideas about the guru. It questions how will it exclusively get this wisdom from the guru.

However, the guru doesn't make you knowledgeable, but rather makes you Bright-ignorant. Bright (*Tej*) is a word coined to indicate something that transcends the dualities. Bright-ignorant is the one who transcends both knowledge and ignorance. You return to the innocence of a child, where you live in the blissful wonder of "not-knowing" and allow life to unfold.

Your true Self already exists; in truth, your true Self is all that exists! It's just that you have strayed away from the *experience* of the Self. The guru just leads you back to that experience. He breaks all the beliefs, assumptions and notions that are an obstruction to your experience. Your mind becomes open, receptive, and non-assuming. If you have unflinching faith, complete trust and devotion in your guru and you sincerely contemplate on each and every word he speaks, you will find that every word will render deep insight of the inner world. One day, the eureka effect will happen and you will be blessed with the ultimate understanding. You will attain Self-realization.

And, what do you need to do for this to happen? Nothing! You are already that, which you are seeking! Your body is just a medium for that.

Imagine you have a mirror. The sole purpose of the mirror is to show you how you are. Now imagine that the mirror also has its own eyes and its own world. It can see the world through its eyes. In the same way, the body-mind is also like a mirror that helps to make you aware of your own presence, your sense of being. While the body-mind is experiencing the world, it is also helping you to know yourself, to make you aware of your nature.

Who we truly are is separate from the body. The guru just makes you aware that you are not the mirror. The mirror is merely an instrument which needs to be used to realize your true Self, your true nature.

8
The State of Complete Surrender

Seeker A: I want to know how I can attain the state of complete surrender? What do I need to do for that?

Sirshree: In order to attain the state of complete surrender, an earnest truth-seeking disciple needs to have Bright-faith, Bright-trust and Bright-love for his guru. Bright-faith is beyond both doubt and faith. Bright-trust transcends trust and distrust. Bright-love is unconditional; it is beyond both love and hatred. When complete surrender happens, one starts doubting his own doubter-mind. The mind tends to doubt everything and ironically, we never doubt the doubting mind itself!

Here, it's important to understand who needs to attain the state of complete surrender. The mind, which has assumed itself to be separate from everything else, needs to surrender. When the mind surrenders, there remains nothing for it to do anymore. With the dissolution of the mind, comes the disappearance of personalized thoughts, and once this happens, the truth that is shrouded behind thoughts is revealed.

Seeker B: Can you please elaborate?

Sirshree: Let's understand it with the help of a story:

Once upon a time, there lived a king. He believed that the only way he could earn an entry to heaven after his death was to perform a hundred *yagnas* (a ritual performed by chanting mantras before a sacred fire) during his lifetime. Per his belief, he had been organizing grand *yagnas* in his kingdom and had already completed ninety-two of the total hundred that he wished to perform.

He indiscriminately spent the money from the kingdom's treasury to cater to his personal whims instead of the welfare of the subjects. The subjects, completely unaware of this, were busy enjoying the pomp. They were happily partaking in the *yagnas* and enjoying the foods, sweets and gifts that were being distributed. The whole kingdom was in grand celebration.

While the king was busy with the *yagnas,* his guru was away on account of being in a meditative trance. As soon as he emerged from his trance, he thought of his disciple.

The guru remembers his disciple in two situations: either when the disciple has lost his way and strayed off the path of truth, or when the disciple has prepared himself for the further journey.

He immediately came to know that the king had lost his way. He realized that the king had entangled himself in a web of misconceptions and was plundering the kingdom's treasury. It was necessary to meet him and shake him out of his reverie.

With this purpose in mind, the guru reached the ritual site in the disguise of an ordinary ascetic. After he had food, the king approached him, "O great saint, what can I offer you as alms?"

The guru replied, "Are you really prepared to give me whatever I ask for?"

"Of course," said the king, who now had the confidence of having completed the hundred *yagnas*. "You just have to express your wish, and I shall fulfil it."

The guru vehemently repeated with loud intensity, "Well then, whatever is yours is mine from now on."

The king was shocked at such a demand, but it was a tradition that once given, one had to keep his word for the entire lifetime at any cost. Accordingly, the king conceded to the guru's wish, "Whatever is mine is yours from now on."

As per tradition, someone who accepted alms also deserved to be given a gift for accepting the alms. This was because they were doing a great favor upon the giver by accepting the alms, by giving him an opportunity to perform a sanctified deed.

Accordingly, the guru asked for a gift in return for having accepted the alms from the king. The king thought hard for a moment about what else he could give the ascetic now. After much thought, the king started to remove his necklace to offer as a gift.

The guru immediately stopped him and said, "What are you doing, O king? You can't offer me that necklace! You are forgetting that whatever is yours is now mine. So that necklace is already mine. You can't offer me something that is already mine!"

The king was dumbfounded, "Yes, he is right! The necklace isn't mine anymore! My kingdom, my soldiers, the ministers, my palace, none of it belongs to me anymore!"

As he was lost in thoughts, the guru's words fell upon his ears, "You have given me everything of yours. Hence, your mind also belongs to me. How can you think without my permission?"

This gave a sudden jolt to the king, "I can't think without permission." His thoughts suddenly ceased and he was catapulted to a timeless state beyond thoughts – the state which one experiences when one is in deep sleep, except that he was consciously aware of it.

While in the trance, the king found himself standing in Indra's court. Addressing him, Indra – the king of gods – said, "The balance sheet of your sins and virtues has been scrutinized. As you have earned more virtues, you deserve to enjoy heavenly pleasures. However, you have committed some sins too, on account of which, you have to endure hell for a short while. Now, it's up to you, which one you would like to experience first – the pleasure of your good deeds or the pain of your bad deeds?"

The king thought for a while and decided to get done with the sufferings of hell first and then enjoy heaven.

Accordingly, he found himself wandering aimlessly in the middle of a hot desert. Thirsty and tired, he kept walking, but couldn't see a single drop of water. The desolate desert stretched as far as his eyes could see.

He then suddenly remembered, "Why am I enduring the

sufferings of hell? If I have given everything to the ascetic, then how can the sins be mine?" As soon as this enlightening thought occurred to him, the king found himself in heaven!

Now, the king went into deep contemplation, "If the sins are not mine, then how can the virtues be mine?" He transcended the dualities of heaven and hell, sins and virtues, joy and sorrow, success and failure. He was now free from all illusion and experiencing the bliss of the ultimate truth. As his eyes opened, he saw his guru standing before him, smiling benevolently at his satisfied disciple!

So now, what did you gather from this story?

Seeker A: Attaining heaven is something that comes in the realm of mental prowess, it has nothing to do with performing *yagnas*. One could perform a hundred thousand *yagnas* and still not be able to transcend his mind and attain heavenly bliss.

Sirshree: That's right.

Seeker B: Through a small experiment, the guru freed the king of his illusions and misbeliefs. It's very easy to abandon the tortures of hell as everyone wants to get away from them, but it's difficult to let go off the pleasures of heaven. It's not the rituals, or money, or food, but rather, it is complete surrender that matters the most to experience true bliss.

Sirshree: That's true! One can attain a thoughtless state only when one is conscious and awakened. The king had Bright-faith on his guru. Hence, just one instruction from the guru was enough for him to completely surrender his doubting mind and attain the experience of the Self.

Seeker A: Then what makes this so difficult?

Sirshree: The devious vacillating mind and the extreme simplicity of the truth, together make the truth very difficult to grasp.

The contrast mind believes that it is going to receive the truth. Hence, it tries to predetermine and pre-fix how enlightenment will occur in terms of whatever happens at the body-mind level. It wants to be present to witness how the Self realizes itself and tries imagining it. However, there is nothing for the mind to know. True surrender is about being in the bliss of "not knowing". Only when the mind surrenders that the true Self shines.

But the mind fears the unknown and always wants to hold onto something that is known to survive. It doesn't want to lose its identity. Hence, it makes it difficult for the mind to completely surrender itself.

9
The Paths Leading to the Truth

Seeker A: I have heard that there are various paths to progress towards enlightenment. What are they?

Sirshree: There are many paths that lead to abiding in the Self, such as *Gyana* (Wisdom), *Dhyana* (Meditation), *Karma* (Action) and *Bhakti* (Devotion).

Seeker A: Amongst these paths, which path is more effective?

Sirshree: All the paths that are known in spirituality finally culminate in a two-fold path – one approach is that of wisdom, while the other is that of devotion.

Seeker B: I have heard about the path of devotion. People who tread this path praise the lord and sing hymns.

Sirshree: The path of devotion is the path of surrender to the divine will of God. It is the path of submitting to Consciousness – the Source of everything. Effort in this path is effortless, as actions happen in joyous surrender to the Self.

Once you are immersed in the state of devotion, praise for the lord and singing of hymns happens automatically. However, people assume mere external actions to be devotion itself and imitate them. But true devotion happens only after one internally surrenders oneself in the service to the lord.

Seeker B: That's a great insight. The external expression of devotion has to be preceded by true surrender internally. And what is the path of wisdom?

Sirshree: The path of wisdom is that of intellectual reasoning and meditation. On this path, the seeker of truth uses his will power and applies his intellect to grasp the truth and internalize it.

Seeker A: Can you please elaborate these paths?

Sirshree: The path of devotion is akin to the way of a kitten, which leaves its body loose and gives itself up to its mother, who then carries it around with her mouth. The path of wisdom is like the way of a baby monkey that needs to clasp onto its mother's belly when she jumps from one branch to the other. The kitten surrenders. The baby monkey clutches with all its might.

Seeker A: That's a striking example.

Seeker B: But if the intended result of walking both these paths is the same, how do these distinct paths lead to the same result?

Sirshree: Good question! Let's understand this with the help of an example. There were two travelers who needed to cross safely through a jungle to return home. One of them was blind, while the other did not have legs. Individually, they could not have made it home. The lame traveler climbed onto the shoulders of his blind companion and started guiding him through the jungle. The blind man followed his directions and walked carefully, carrying him through the jungle. In this way, both managed to reach home safely.

So it is on the path of Self-realization. The lame man symbolizes the eye of wisdom, while the blind one represents the legs of devotion. Without the legs of devotion, the eyes of wisdom cannot walk the path. And the legs of devotion cannot see the path without the eyes of wisdom. Let devotion obtain the eyes of wisdom and let wisdom in turn receive the legs of devotion.

The seeker who pursues the path of wisdom through the practice of meditation and conscious *karma* develops unswerving faith, thereby leading to the surrender of his individual personhood to the Self. The one who follows the path of devotion matures in understanding of the truth.

Finally, the one who works on gaining wisdom surrenders, and the one who surrenders attains wisdom. Thus, both the paths merge at its culmination in Self-realization.

Seeker B: Wow! This analogy is so apt to explain how the two paths complement each other! So then, how do I start? Which path do I choose to start the journey?

Sirshree: You do not have to decide which path is best for you. Whatever the mind prefers need not be the best path for you. Following the path that the mind feels like is like asking a thief how he would like to be captured. The thief would never give away the path that would lead to his downfall. Similarly, the aspect of the mind that considers itself as a separate individual has to drop. That aspect of the mind cannot be trusted to decide which path to tread.

Leave how this happens to grace. Ultimately, grace is the only way. When a true guru enters the seeker's life, the light of grace propels the seeker on the path that is most suited to him or her. The presence of the guru is essential on both the paths.

Seeker A: How does the guru help in this journey?

Sirshree: On the path of wisdom, the guru guides the disciple on how he should meditate. He points him in the right direction and gives him appropriate points to contemplate. The disciple then contemplates and does self-reflection. He uses his own intellect and logic to understand his body-mind and seek his true Self, till a point where he realizes the limit of his intellect. He realizes that the true Self cannot be perceived by the intellect and that it comes in the realm of experience.

As soon as the seeker on the path of wisdom realizes the futility of his efforts to assimilate the ultimate wisdom through the intellect, he also realizes that the entity that was seeking the truth, the one who was self-reflecting, the one who was looking for answers, is itself non-existent! That "Eureka!" moment leads him to surrender his intellect and logic, and catapults him into the realm of experience, wherein the true Self is revealed.

On the path of devotion, the guru imparts understanding and instructs you as per the nature of your body-mind. You remain in the presence of the guru, become receptive to his guidance. When you completely and doubtlessly surrender to the natural flow of life as guided by the guru, the ego that considers itself separate from everything else dissolves.

Thus, on both the paths, the guru becomes instrumental for the annihilation of the individual ego of the disciple and leads him to a state of total surrender – which is the utmost important attribute to prepare one for the final truth.

As surrender is so very important, various religious scriptures have words like *"Let Thy will be done", "Inshallah", "Hukum"* all of which mean surrender to the will of God.

Seeker B: It is true that without complete surrender, one cannot realize the final truth. But when one has a heavy intellect and logical mind, one may find it difficult to surrender the mind. In such a situation how can one proceed in his journey?

Sirshree: Let's understand this with the help of a story:

A flock of swans lived on a large tree deep in a forest. There was a vine plant at the bottom of the tree that slowly crept its way up on the tree's trunk. An old and wise swan also lived in this group.

One day the old swan told the other swans, "You need to uproot the vine plant on an urgent basis."

The swans nodded to him in agreement and told, "We will surely work upon it tomorrow." They then continued with their routine. They would play, travel from place to place, rejoice and return by evening. Thus, days passed by but they didn't work upon his advice.

After a few days, the vine plant that twirled around the stem grew up to reach the very top of the trunk where the swans lived. The old swan knew that anyone could climb up the tree using this creeper as support and cause nuisance to the swans. He recognized the grave danger the swans were in, since hunters often came to the forest and captured the birds.

One fine day, a hunter found his way up on the tree with the help of the fully-grown vine plant. He climbed the tree and spread his net to capture the swans. Unfortunately, the old swan was out-of-tree that day due to some work.

When the old swan returned and found that all the other swans were captured, he immediately visualized the entire incident. The netted swans saw the old swan and pleaded for help, "Please save us. Please help us. We're all captured."

But, instead of providing any help, the old swan angrily lashed out at them.

"I reminded you plenty of times. You should have taken my advice and uprooted the creeper well in time. See what has happened now!" said the old swan, "This is exactly what you deserve."

The swans were extremely surprised at the old swan's odd behavior. He was otherwise very calm by nature and had never once uttered a harsh word before.

But the old bird went on and his temper refused to go down. "You all deserve to die like this. No one can save you now."

The swans cried and begged for their lives. They knew that if someone could help them at all, it was the old swan. After a lot of persuasion, the old swan agreed to help them on one condition.

"You should do *exactly* as I say. One little mistake and I would never help you again in any way."

The swans agreed unanimously. They didn't want to die.

The old swan then whispered the plan.

"The hunter will return tomorrow to collect his captives. When he finds you in the net, all you need to do is to remain still and unmoved, as if you are dead.

"Don't move a part. Dare not make a sound. Act as if you are not in the body. Let your body loose, as if you are in deep meditation." And the old bird went on.

"Finding you dead, the hunter will then release you and fling you on the ground. Don't dare to fly when you are tossed on the ground. Stay still at the place where you fall. Don't move an inch.

"Keep lying as if you are in deep meditation and count your breath. The hunter will then toss all of you on the ground, one by one. Count the sounds of each swan's fall in your heart. Pay full attention. One…two…three… and exactly when you hear the last member falling, you should all fly together, immediately. This is the only way for you to regain your freedom!"

The swans did exactly what was told to them. They rested still and kept counting the falling sounds of each swan hitting the ground. Finally, when the last one hit the ground, all of them flew away together in an instant.

The hunter was shocked. He couldn't comprehend what happened. Frustrated, he collected his net and left the tree.

The swans cheered at their victory and continued to lead a merry life once again. This incident taught them a lesson and they now obeyed everything that the old bird said.

But they still felt puzzled about one thing. They could not understand the reason behind the old swan's odd behavior when they were captured.

One day they asked him, "Why were you so angry that day? We never imagined that even you could be angry."

The old swan then disclosed the secret. Laughing, he said, "It wasn't anger. It was merely an act!

"I was only acting. If I hadn't done so, then I knew you would not stick to my advice and would surely make a mistake. The hunter would then know about your plan and only couple of you would make it outside. Hence I wanted to ensure that all of you should escape. To achieve this, I deliberately used a mask of rage."

So, what did you learn from this story?

Seeker B: The swans failed to realize that the old swan was advising them for their own good. Hence, they ignored his advice. It's only when they were trapped that they were ready to listen to him and follow his illogical advice. At the end, with team work they flew away to freedom.

Seeker A: Now, I understand the importance of abiding by the instructions of the guru. Not a single letter uttered by the guru is ever futile. Every word coming from him should be contemplated deeply and followed till the very last. Sometimes, he may pretend to be harsh but it's only for the wellbeing of the disciples.

Sirshree: That's right! We believe ourselves to be the limited body-mind and behave according to the whims and fancies of the mind, get attached to its desires, just like what the swans did. When we give in to the whims of the mind, we get entangled in their trap and bring misery upon ourselves.

Seeker B: When we get ready to abide by the guru's instructions even when our intellect and logical mind are not in agreement with what's being told, our individual ego gets annihilated. I can see that unshaken faith, courage, devotion, wisdom and love play an important role in this journey.

When we not only abide by the guru's advice but also apply it in our life, we experientially know who we truly are. We then transcend the body-mind and get stabilized in the experience of the Self. This is the only true way to our salvation.

Sirshree: Yes. You have decoded the message well!

Seeker A: I now understand the importance of abiding by the guru's words. I had a question regarding the paths to the truth that you explained earlier. I have heard about the path of Self-enquiry that helps us transcend the false "I" and experience the true Self. Does this practice of Self-enquiry belong in the path of wisdom?

Sirshree: The path of Self-enquiry is the approach of negating who you are *not,* so that what remains is who you truly are. This approach starts from the Self. All other practices start from enquiry of the body-mind, where you try to learn more about the body and mind. These two methods are another paradigm of approaching the journey to truth.

Seeker B: Can you please elaborate these methods?

Sirshree: Most of the seekers of truth, who do not have a guide or a guru, choose the path of the body-mind to begin their spiritual journey. They believe themselves to be the body, mind and intellect and strive hard to perfect them. As the results are tangible and quantifiable, they are encouraged to become better and better.

They improve their power of concentration, self-confidence, listening skills. However, there is a risk of getting lured by the powers and miracles of the body-mind. One may get stuck in practices such as awakening one's *chakras*, breath-work, etc. in the name of spirituality. Thus, one may abandon progressing on one's spiritual journey.

Seeker A: What happens with the path of Self-enquiry?

Sirshree: People who start on the path of Self-enquiry, dive into the fundamental existential question, "Who am I?" In and through each and every situation, they enquire, "Whose story is going on? Mine. If it is 'my' story, then who am I?" If they get angry, then they question, "Who is feeling angry? Me. Who is this 'me'?" Thus, consistent contemplation on this question leads them to the real Self.

However, there is no way to find out exactly how much they have progressed on the path of Self-enquiry; neither are there any quantitative measures. Hence, they may get doubtful whether they are making any progress at all and abandon the practice.

Seeker B: Which path should one choose to start with?

Sirshree: If one is left free to choose one's path, he would make the choice as per his tendencies, comfort zone and temperament of the body-mind. People whose body-mind has a temperament of *tamas*, will tend to be lacklustre, dull and apathetic. They need to choose the path of body-mind training in order to overcome their lethargy. However, ironically most of them choose the path of Self-enquiry as it allows them to remain in their comfort-zone.

They become monks and hermits, thinking that will put them on the direct and shortest path to Self-realization, without taking all the effort of working on their body-mind to improve their skills, abilities and health. They escape from their homes and lead a life of asceticism. For many people who choose to become hermits, it isn't the apt path for them at all. They ought to follow the path of body-mind training, but their lethargic tendency compels them to choose otherwise. They want to escape their responsibilities and this path becomes their excuse.

The path of self-enquiry is the perfect alternative for people with the temperament of *sattva* as they have balanced tendencies. They are neither too active nor too lethargic.

Seeker B: What is the way out of this? How would we know whether we are following the path that we ought to, and not what our tendencies dictate?

Sirshree: The guru guides the disciple to walk on both the paths simultaneously as per the temperament of his body-mind. Initially the disciple may follow it half-heartedly, with a sense of helpless obligation. However, when even the half-hearted application begets positive changes in his life, he realizes the importance of the seemingly needless instructions and preparation that the guru had him go through.

By following the path of Self-enquiry, the disciple realizes his true nature. His level of awareness rises. On every troubling thought, when he conducts Self-enquiry, he learns the art of leading a relaxed and centred life.

By training his body-mind, his perseverance, alertness and concentration increases. He gains mastery over his sense organs. Even if he commits mistakes due to wrong decisions, he learns to convert them for his good. Thus, by utilizing benefits of both the paths, he becomes independent in a true sense. His body-mind helps him to stay in the experience of the Self and express its qualities and limitless potential.

10
Significance of the Guru-Disciple Relationship

Seeker A: One of my colleagues filed for divorce. She was not getting along with her husband. I was reflecting on the fragility of human relationships and wondering how relationships between partners can be so brittle. In my experience, the bond between parents and children, even siblings', can be so strong.

Sirshree: (laughs) It's because you have accepted them since you were an infant and have stopped looking at them consciously or contemplating over the reasons why they exist. They have become so deep rooted that you take them for granted and never think about severing them.

However, you consciously form relationships with your spouse and friends. As adults, when a man and a woman decide to tie the knot, they consciously accept each other. In friendship too, you accept your friend consciously. Such relationships are based on understanding and acceptance. Therefore, if they find that their coming together is not mutually helping each other, they may even consider separating, as it is happening all the more these days.

Seeker B: That's right! During college days, I had a close friend. We used to meet up frequently and continued the same even after we started working. On one of her birthdays, I was in the midst of my busy work schedule and forgot to wish her. After a few days, when I tried to call her, she didn't respond. Later, she messaged me on my birthday, "If I remember your birthday, I expect you to remember mine." I tried to explain my viewpoint but in vain. She wasn't in the frame to give me a patient hearing. Thereafter, we parted our ways. It was sad to know that our relationship was not based on love and trust but it was based on expectations.

Seeker A: Even one of my friends asked me to join him in his business venture. When I denied the offer, he stopped interacting with me. Our long friendship came to an end.

Sirshree: Most of these relationships are based on expectations, ego, hatred, jealousy, anger, lust and greed. Even the love expressed in these relationships is largely selfish and conditional, because the underlying sentiment is, "I have done a lot for you and hence I expect you to do the same." Failure to fulfil expectations leads to strained relationships. A relationship that is vulnerable to such displeasures, never exists in the first place.

Seeker B: That's true! Due to my busy work schedule, many a times I am unable to attend family functions and my relatives get upset. They deduce that I don't love or respect them anymore. They fail to understand the reason for my absence and my love for them. I seriously feel that almost all relationships are based on expectations; they are conditional. Having said this, I wonder whether the relationship with the guru is also conditional. Do we need to reciprocate in some kind for what we receive from the guru?

Sirshree: The relationship with the guru is different from other relationships. Let us understand how.

The very first relationship you have is with your mother, while you are being nurtured in her womb. At that time, you are in a state akin to that of *Samadhi* – a timeless state of being.

As soon as you are born in the world, you form the second kind of relationships – blood relations – father, brother, sister, uncles, aunts, grandparents, etc.

Later in life, you make friends. You choose your companion, your life partner. These are the third kind of relationships.

The ultimate relationship is with your guru. This has been called the greatest relationship of all, because you consciously attain the original state of the true Self in the presence of the guru. The guru guides you through this process and gives you complete understanding.

Unlike other relationships, this relationship is formed in an ascended state of consciousness. When the disciple, sincerely seeking the greatest benefaction ever, meets the guru, who is the greatest benefactor ever (the ultimate giver), there is a deep and profound attraction towards each other. The greatest demand one can ever make is that of the ultimate truth, the very purpose for which he is born.

Seeker B: Usually I am a little hesitant in asking something from someone. So, I'm not sure how or even whether I can ask for the greatest attainment.

Sirshree: An honest and sincere truth-seeker feels no hesitation or reluctance in expecting nothing but the ultimate truth from the guru. Hesitation is only felt with other relations, not with the guru. Hesitation forms a wall that separates people from one another. Even minor fallouts cause people to stop talking to each other for years. Owing to such hesitation and ego, neither person wants to take the first step towards re-establishing communication. Each one wants the other person to initiate and break the ice.

The guru-disciple relation is free of all hesitations and ego. Both, the giver and the seeker, have a strong affinity towards each other. Hence it's considered to be the greatest of all relations. It is beyond all the other relations you shall have in your life. It takes some time to understand this relationship, but once you do, you are absolved of all your sorrows and worldly illusions.

Unlike other relationships, this supreme relationship is completely unconditional. Even if you are unable to reciprocate your love towards the guru in any form, the relationship still continues. The flow of unconditional love from the guru never stops. Hence, this relationship is also called a divine relationship and has the ability to transform you and change your life.

Seeker A: Can one approach his guru as a friend, or a father?

Sirshree: You can have any relationship with your guru, but don't expect him to reciprocate in the same manner. When you consider yourself as the child of the guru and the guru as your father, you need to understand that all the problems start as soon as you ascribe a label to any relationship. You expect him to cater to your demands. You prefer to receive guidance as per your own customs and methods. You feel, "I prefer this particular way, therefore I should receive the knowledge in this way alone." Thus, your mind starts guiding you. Therefore, the guru asks you to keep aside the judging mind and listen without any preconceived notions. At least in this way, the mind can surrender.

When you consider yourself a friend of the guru, the inherent limitations and expectations of friendship come into play. You very well know how you behave with your friends. You might expect the same from the guru. You listen to your friend as per your stipulations of time and expectations. Friends generally tend to interact with each other at a superficial level; such friendships lack intensity or depth.

Hence, consider the guru as your Bright friend. Bright friend is the one who transcends both friendship and enmity. Your friends may turn into enemies, but your Bright friend will remain your friend and well-wisher, no matter what.

As a matter of fact, attributing any label to the relationship between the guru and the disciple is like representing a vast, deep concept or principle in a single word. Therefore, this relationship cannot be described in words. You can take it both ways – either this relationship should not be assigned a label, or this relationship should encompass all relationships. Therefore, this relationship can also be called the Bright relationship.

From the guru's viewpoint, there is no relationship, as the guru does not consider his disciple to be separate from him. For him, there is no separation or otherness. If there is no "other" (separate individual), then how can there be a relationship? However, from the disciple's viewpoint, the relationship still exists as this is the only relationship that enables him to transcend all names and forms, and makes it possible for him to break the ego and attain liberation.

Seeker B: But I still don't understand why the guru can't follow worldly relationships in the way others do, if not always, at least for some time?

Sirshree: Understand the purpose behind the guru's existence in your life. He is here to free you of your illusions, not to entertain them and make them stronger. He is here to disrupt your slumber, not deepen it. His conduct is not aimed towards pleasing you, but towards your eternal benefit. When you understand the guru's ways, you stop questioning them. You will then focus on the purpose and the teaching of the guru instead of raising doubts over his attire, language and conduct. His actions will then make perfect sense.

There has to be someone in your life, who speaks to your true Self; who takes you for who you truly are, not who you project yourself to be. You have so far mistaken your body, mind or intellect to be your Self and hence, you may also regard your guru from the same perspective. You've mistaken the limited knowledge you've gathered through your senses to be the ultimate wisdom. Someone has to disrupt this illusion. Your guru is here to awaken you. Whatever he says or does, however hurtful it may seem to the judging mind, comes from unconditional love. The guru is interacting with your true Self, and all dealings with the true Self spring from eternal love.

In life, the guru is indeed a light of grace who speaks to who you truly are, not your projected individual self. When you realize the importance of this grace, you will be filled with the deepest gratitude for it. This is the greatest blessing of all. A human mind is often incapable of even recognizing grace. You are surrounded by things that could be nothing but true blessings, but ironically you might fail to appreciate them. You form your own impressions about how and what you want a blessing to be. The guru however disrupts all such impressions and illusions and bestows on you the one true blessing – realization of your true Self.

Only the guru-disciple relationship can transform you, elevate you. Hence it can be termed as a divine relationship. Help your guru to help you stabilize in the experience of your true Self.

Seeker A: How does the guru-disciple relationship mature?

Sirshree: In the beginning, the new seeker approaches the guru to observe and evaluate him. He tests the guru's knowledge. At this stage, the relationship between them is like that between a teacher and a student.

When the guru discusses various topics with such a novice student, the relationship is limited to arguments. Conclusions are drawn from intellectual discussions and debates. The student wants to learn something from the guru, but he is yet only aspiring to gain knowledge.

Gradually, the student transforms into a sincere seeker. Having transformed into a seeker, he starts enquiring into his true identity "Who am I?" His quest for the truth intensifies. After a while, the seeking ends and the seeker is transformed into the guru's disciple. This is surrender.

The disciple then evolves into a devotee. His love, faith and trust in the guru matures. The journey culminates when the devotee transcends into divinity. It is now that Guru, God, Grace and the devotee become one. There remains no separateness between them.

Seeker A: I have heard about the guru-disciple relationship between Swami Vivekananda and Ramakrishna Paramhansa.

Sirshree: Ramakrishna Paramhansa was an extraordinary guru, and Swami Vivekananda was an exemplary disciple. While the master reveled in the bliss of the heart, the disciple delighted in intellectual heights. It was a unique combination that makes this pair exceptional.

Vivekananda was a determined and persevering seeker of truth. Whoever he met, he would ask, "Have you seen God?" When he met Ramakrishna Paramhansa, he asked him the same question. Instead of answering his question with a "Yes" or a "No", Ramakrishna Paramhansa grabbed him by his neck and exclaimed, "Let me *show* you God. I cannot answer your question in words, so let me show you instead!" Vivekananda had an earnest urge for knowing the truth, and when he met the greatest giver, his guru, he got to experience the truth in his life.

Stories of Saint Dnyaneshwar and Saint Nivruttinath, Saint Meera and Saint Rohidaas, Guru Nanak and Guru Angad are all similar and have the same message: When the urge to acquire the final truth takes root in a disciple, the Guru has to appear in his life to bestow the ultimate wisdom. When the Guru enters his life, his life blossoms with divine strength and devotion.

11
Training the Body, Mind and Intellect

Seeker A: In today's hi-tech world, people are trapped in the lure of illusions. Television, radio, newspapers, films, social media are all propagating illusions and people find it hard to resist the charm.

To quench your thirst, you are asked to drink a certain cold drink instead of water. You are constantly being told that you are not healthy enough or beautiful enough, and that you need to use certain products to keep up with the ways of the world. The habits and tendencies we have developed since our childhood make us extremely vulnerable to these illusory indulgences. When a seeker comes from such a background, how does the guru work on him?

Sirshree: Before we discuss this, first answer this question.

A yard used to be full of weeds. Nothing else would grow, not even grass. The soil had lots of stones in it. How would you transform the yard from a weed wasteland to a vegetable garden?

Seeker A: I don't know how this question is related to my question. But let me try to answer.

I'll first remove the stones from the soil. Then I'll pull out the weeds from their roots. After that I'll water the soil to make it soft. Once it's done, I'll plough the soil and sow seeds in it. With sufficient supply of water, fertilizer and sunlight, it will soon grow into a vegetable garden.

Sirshree: You've answered your own question very well.

Seeker A: I didn't get you.

Sirshree: The guru first removes the stones of your inherent beliefs. He then pulls out the deeply rooted weeds of tendencies and habits. Thereafter, he ploughs the soil of the mind and nurtures it with the light of grace and the water of faith. Once, the mind becomes receptive, he sows the wholesome seeds of ultimate wisdom in it. Thus, before the guru sows the ultimate wisdom, he first prepares you for it.

Seeker B: Wow! That's a wonderful comparison to the example of the vegetable garden. Can you please elaborate further?

Sirshree: As your body-mind is not trained, you fall victim to the lures of the material world. Therefore, the guru teaches you to love yourself. Now, what do you understand when you are told to love yourself?

Seeker B: I always feel when someone assists me in my work, gratifies my wishes, makes my stay comfortable, talks to me in a sweet tone, respects me, and cares for me, then they love me.

Seeker A: When I was a child, we had to practice lot of craftwork.

After finishing with school homework, I used to feel tired. Then sometimes my mom used to complete my craftwork. I used to feel loved when she would do my craftwork.

Sirshree: It's very common to feel that we are being loved when the demands of our body, mind and intellect are fulfilled. But we fail to understand that such love doesn't make us self-sufficient. It just gratifies the wants of our senses. Such love makes us dependent on people. We are then subject to the dualities of joy-sorrow, success-failure, honor-dishonor in our life.

When the guru enters our life, he imparts the right understanding and teaches the art of loving ourselves. He teaches us how to master our body, mind and intellect. Instead of becoming their slaves, we shower them with loving care only as much as is due to them. Thereafter self-discipline becomes an integral part of our life. With self-discipline, we finish our work in time and with quality. All worldly achievements, success, and joy become part of our life.

Once, we gain mastery over our body, mind and intellect, we become proficient to tread on the path towards the ultimate goal of life. It's like we first polish the shoes and then embark on our journey.

Seeker B: I never considered that our body, mind and intellect need to be trained separately. I would like to know more about it.

Sirshree: While training our body, mind and intellect, we need to give fatherly love to our body, motherly love to our mind and the guru's love to our intellect.

Seeker B: What is this fatherly, motherly and the guru's love? I couldn't understand anything.

Sirshree: (laughs) Okay. Let's understand it step by step.

Fatherly love is the epitome of tough love. So, while training your body, be tough with it. A father in the family inculcates the habit of exercises in his children and compels them to get up early in the morning. Children don't like to get up early. Mothers also support them and insist that the father shouldn't be hard on them. But the determined father makes them wake up, and follow a daily regimen.

Seeker B: (laughs) It has happened with me when I was a kid. I used to hate the disciplined ways of my father. I used to question why I can't sleep for whatever time I feel like on holidays. I used to take it like a torture when my father used to wake me up. My body used to resist strongly.

Seeker A: Even when my father used to make me do exercises, I used to feel that I am being punished.

Sirshree: Hmm. As a child you won't like fatherly love. But when you develop self-discipline in your life as a result, you appreciate how truly your father loved you. When your body becomes trained, you understand how essential fatherly love was.

Now, you need to give this tough fatherly love to your own body. When you realize who you truly are, you won't shy away from taking intentions to exercise your body as well as perform *pranayama*. But ensure that you do it in the right proportion. Else, if you get into the other extreme of over-working the body, it could cause pain to your body. Understand that a painful body doesn't support you. You need a healthy and fit body for your expression.

Seeker B: What kind of intentions do I need to take to exercise my body?

Sirshree: When we talk about training the body, it also constitutes training the senses. The sense organs are the eyes, ears, nose, tongue, and skin, which cater to the senses of vision, sound, smell, taste and speech, and touch respectively. In order to train these sense organs, you may start your day with new intentions every day. For example, you may take intentions like speaking politely in a soft tone, or observe fasting, or not to watch TV, or not to engage in gossip, or leaving some portion of your favorite dish, etc. With consistent practice, you can develop self-discipline on your body and sense organs.

Seeker B: I will surely practice this.

Sirshree: There is a word of caution though. After gaining control over your body, at any point in time, if you gratify the craving of any of your senses in excess, your love vanishes and lust takes over.

Also, after developing mastery over your body, if you utilise the power of intention to attain occult powers that bloat your ego, then the feeling of love will vanish and you will develop arrogance and the air of superiority.

Seeker A: I will be vigilant so that I don't fall a prey to these so-called spiritual allurements. You also mentioned about motherly love. I wanted to know how motherly love helps to train the mind.

Sirshree: Motherly love is the epitome of unconditional, unlimited, and undoubting love. You are reminded of compassion and gratitude with motherly love. A bumble bee keeps moving from one flower to another in search of nectar. Likewise, our mind keeps wandering from one topic to another in search of happiness, thereby draining our energy in the process. Such a restless mind cannot remain focussed on a single topic for long and thus cannot help us in attaining our ultimate goal.

We need to train our mind to become unshakable, obedient, pure and loving. When motherly love is rendered to the mind, it calms down, wholeheartedly accepts whatever is happening and gets immersed in devotion. Thereafter, it becomes receptive to higher wisdom and gets ready to surrender to the divine will of God. In the process, you get enriched with qualities like patience, perseverance, forgiveness, gratitude, compassion, determination and devotion.

But ensure that you love your mind in the right proportion. When the mind likes to get into allurements and distractions of the world, re-focus it on the bliss of devotion. Without devotion, it will rebel against you. Thus, strike the right balance by neither getting attached to it, nor making it rebel. At no point in time should you permit your mind to become your master, you always remain its master and let it be your faithful servant.

Seeker B: If the body and mind both get trained then what kind of training does the guru impart to the intellect?

Sirshree: The guru imparts ultimate wisdom with which the intellect gains higher perspective, flexibility and devotion. Your discerning power strengthens. Instead of looking for solutions to a problem, you view the problem with the new perspective and find that the solution is already there. Thus, you learn the art of turning roadblocks into stepping stones and progress in your journey. In the process, the power of acceptance and devotion will awaken within you and you will be freed from your wrong habits and tendencies. With the ultimate wisdom that you receive from the guru, you can experientially realize who you truly are.

The guru teaches you to learn every day, learn from every mistake, learn new things from new mistakes. The day you fail to learn anything, you have wasted your day. You have lost the opportunity to work on yourself. When you learn every day, take intentions and work on them, you master your body. You can then consider your body as a friend and utilize it for your highest expression.

Seeker A: This is impressive! People try to escape working on their body or mind under the garb of false spirituality. I can see how the right way of loving ourselves can train and transform our body, mind and intellect. This is true wisdom, indeed!

Sirshree: However, there is an inherent risk in the words of wisdom. You may get stuck in those words and consider yourself to be one with supreme wisdom. Despite gaining the highest wisdom, it is possible to remain deprived of its essence. You will remain the most ignorant of all. Hence, you need to grasp the essence of those words and realize your true nature. Then abandon those words, once the words have served their true purpose of conveying the essential knowledge to you.

Seeker B: I never thought that love and self-discipline are so deeply related with each other.

Sirshree: When the body, mind and intellect are deprived of self-discipline and love, they remain distracted and follow different directions. They become the cause of sorrow. But with training, as you nurture love and self-discipline, they become unified, bringing you the experience of bliss.

12
The Guru's Attention

Seeker A: Usually, whenever we are looking for something, we know what we are looking for and have specific details about it. This information helps us search for it. For example, if we lose our watch, we can search for it as we know about its brand, color and model.

But this is not the case with the search for the truth. We don't know how the truth is and yet we are searching for it. Sometimes, I really feel perplexed that we are looking for something without knowing anything about it.

Sirshree: It's true! But this is exactly what happens in the quest for truth. When one sets out, or rather sets *in*, on this inward journey, he is exactly in this dilemma. He knows nothing about the truth and yet he looks for it. He yearns for it. This is where the role of the guru comes into play. Seeking the truth while knowing nothing about it seems like an arduous task. The guru showers his attention on the seeker, guiding him along the way by his mere presence.

Seeker B: But how can the guru guide the various seekers when they may not be even available in his presence?

Sirshree: The guru provides appropriate guidance as per the seekers' nature. The guru uses various methods, each specific to a particular seeker, to make him progress further on the path of truth.

The seeker is made to search for the truth despite the obstacles and distractions of the illusory world. The guru showers his grace and his attention on the seekers in many different ways. Each way is meant for a particular kind of seekers and helps them realize the ultimate goal of Self-realization and Self-stabilization.

Seeker B: What are the different ways by which the guru gives attention to the seekers?

Sirshree: The guru uses various ways of attention to break the seeker's shell of ignorance and ego, and help him realize his true nature.

The first is the way of the turtle. While laying eggs, the turtle emerges from the ocean and lays her eggs safely beneath the soft wet layer of sand. After hiding her eggs safely, the mother returns to the ocean. The hatchlings grow and break out of the tough shell when they are ready. In this process, the eggs hatch even though the mother turtle is far away in the ocean and there is no direct contact between her and the eggs. Similarly, even though the seeker is far away from the guru, the guru's attention remains with the seeker, propelling the seeker on the journey of truth.

Seeker A: Why would the guru use such a method?

Sirshree: There are seekers on whom how the guru's attention works is beyond imagination. Some seekers are available in the presence of the guru while some are not, but the guru's grace embraces them all. It is this potent pure and conscious attention of the guru that helps the seekers break out of the shell of illusion and be born again in the real world.

Seeker A: What's the other way of attention?

Sirshree: The second way is the way of the hen. The hen has a different method of hatching her eggs. The hen doesn't leave her eggs even for a little while. After laying eggs, she sits on them until they become ripe and hatch. This process is called incubation. It is this constant force of love and warmth that helps the eggs hatch.

In the same way, the guru trains a consistent and focused attention on certain other seekers by taking their ego to task relentlessly and delivering knocks. It helps to gradually weaken their ego. It is when the haughty ego dissolves that the true Self can blissfully shine forth.

The guru uses this method for the sincere advanced seekers of the truth so as to annihilate their ego. This method is also used for seekers who are deeply conditioned and are closed from within. They continue with their follies until the guru lashes out at them. The deeply rooted tendencies and habits ingrained in their body-mind during their upbringing pose a hurdle for Self-realization.

Due to certain incidents during childhood, the seeker's heart closes and he feels deprived of love. When such a seeker approaches the guru for the ultimate freedom, the guru guides him to honestly bring out all that has happened with him without any prejudices.

This is for the seeker's own benefit as it helps in bringing one's own mental conditioning to light. When the seeker clearly sees how the body-mind has been conditioned over the years, it is easier to emerge out of the conditioning.

The seeker might say, "My childhood was difficult and abused. Due to those insults and torments, my heart has been bruised and closed. I am unable to feel love for anybody or anything since then. Those injured thoughts of the past keep haunting me and I don't feel at ease. I feel desensitized in situations now and even cannot cry."

Thus by bringing out his so-called story and accepting it wholeheartedly, the seeker takes the first step towards Self-realization. It is the guru's continuous and constant force of grace that liberates him to realize who he truly is, beyond all such conditioning. This force of grace is akin to the caring warmth that the hen lends to its eggs to hatch out of the limiting shell.

Seeker B: Are there any other methods that the guru uses?

Sirshree: Yes, the third method is the power of seeing, the power of visual attention.

In this method, the guru attends to those who are available before him through his seeing. The guru knows and understands the situation of each seeker – the situations that they are coping with, where they get stuck, whether they are really contemplating on the teachings, the extent to which they live as victims of their own past conditioning, how they cater to the whims and fancies of their mind.

This powerful attention from the guru helps break the folly of the seekers.

When birds lay and keep their eggs in their nest, they generally fly nearby them and are available most of the time. They keep looking at the eggs with joy and eagerly wait for them to hatch. Visualization of the hatching of healthy chicks from their eggs is the subject of these birds' attention.

In the same way, the guru checks the purpose behind the seekers' visit and the extent of their true devotion. The purpose should be to raise their level of receptivity and thirst for the truth. Otherwise, when one doesn't know the truth, one doesn't become receptive for the wisdom imparted by the guru. With the constant loving attention of the guru, such seekers break out of their ignorance.

The fourth method is the power of pure presence in devotion. The seekers are not directly in touch with the guru, neither are they given direct attention, yet they are only asked to be available in a receptive state. It is their mere presence with the guru, that makes all the difference.

An ignorant and egoistic seeker might say, "I have been to the spiritual congregation, but no one pays heed to me." But he doesn't realize that he has been asked to be available. This itself is his practice in devotion, his *sadhana*.

Some seekers who have heavy egos and are filled with deceit and doubts may be detained from attending the truth discourses for some time. Such seekers complain about it. But they are told that you have been asked to be only available.

Some birds never pay any direct heed to their eggs but all they do is sing and dance around their nest. There is no direct attention on the eggs. It is only their joyful presence that does the work! This power of presence helps these eggs to hatch. Similarly, devotion and contemplation on the truth is the way for these seekers to remain in the presence of the Guru essence and break the shell of their ego to realize their true Self.

Of all the four methods that we discussed, at least one is applicable to each of the seekers of truth to help break their shell of ignorance and ego, attain Self-realization and stabilize in that experience. With the dawn of truth, the seeker breaks out of the shell of limitations and takes flight in the sky of infinite possibilities; his wings get strengthened. He then doesn't need to depend on anyone for anything. He leads an independent life of true freedom and lets others live the same.

13
Qualities of the Truth-Seeker

Seeker B: What qualities should a seeker of truth have to attain the ultimate truth?

Sirshree: Let's understand it through a story:

An earnest seeker of truth met his guru and disclosed his desire to attain the ultimate truth. He asked the guru, "I want to know who I really am. What should I do?" In order to assess how genuine his quest for truth was, the guru granted him permission to stay at his ashram. He told him, "You can stay here for a year, provided you don't enquire about anything with anyone." The seeker abided by the instruction of the guru and stayed in the ashram for a year.

After a year, he reminded the guru, "O master, as per your instruction, I have stayed in the ashram for a year. Now, please bestow me with wisdom." Looking at his thirst for wisdom, the guru replied, "You will have to contest in a wrestling bout."

A ground was prepared for the bout. The guru knew that the opponent of that disciple was an expert wrestler and the disciple also knew wrestling. The guru deliberately announced, "The one who loses the bout will be sentenced to death."

The disciple was in a dilemma. He thought to himself, "I should not lose the bout, but at the same time I also should not defeat the opponent. If the opponent loses then he will be killed unnecessarily. In any case, one of us has to die. I don't want such outcome."

He fought the bout in such a way that none of them lost. The bout went on for hours. When it was evening, the guru stopped the bout.

This story depicts the qualities that a seeker of truth should develop to attain the ultimate truth. Contemplate on this story and share what qualities you could unravel from the story.

Seeker B: Patience is the first quality, as the disciple waited for a year to gain wisdom from the guru. Otherwise, anyone else would have left it in the pretext of not having all that time.

Sirshree: The mind can't keep itself focussed on one thing for a long time. It gets bored. In an attempt to escape boredom, it tries to derive excitement. It switches from one object to another. It engages itself in some sort of entertainment like watching TV, reading the newspaper, surfing the Internet, or partying with friends. In the process, it vacillates between joy and sorrow, honor and dishonor, praise and blame, victory and defeat. It's incessant rush doesn't help it derive permanent bliss and peace.

When the mind is asked to do nothing, boredom is bound to arise. At such times, enquire within, "Who really is getting bored?" If you get the answer, "Me," then ask, "Who is this

'Me'? Who am I?" Self-enquiry helps one tide through this period of boredom with perseverance. Thereafter, the truth gets the opportunity to emerge.

Seeker A: The second quality could be of 100% listening to the guru and abiding by his instructions. During the one year stay in the ashram, when the disciple was strictly asked not to enquire about anything with anyone, he sincerely followed it. His mind could have given him all reasons to escape the situation, yet he continued to stay.

Even after one year, when he was asked to participate in the contest, he unquestioningly followed the guru's instruction.

The third quality could be perseverance. Until the guru instructed him to stop the bout, he continued with it from morning till evening.

Sirshree: Good. You've identified the qualities well.

Seeker B: The fourth quality could be compassion. The disciple could have defeated his opponent. However, he felt compassion for him. Hence, he fought in such a manner that neither of them got defeated.

The fifth quality could be that of consistent prayer. The guru suddenly created a situation where the disciple had to contest with the opponent. During the wrestling bout, he was continuously praying for higher wisdom as well as safety of the opponent. As a result, he could gain both. His opponent escaped death punishment and he became eligible for gaining higher wisdom from the guru.

Sirshree: Well said! Through this story, you also come to know how the guru functions. The guru guides everyone according to their nature. The need is for a heartfelt prayer for wisdom from the disciple. Hence, one should pray for wisdom and awakening of God within oneself.

Anything else?

Seeker B: Concentration could be the sixth quality. During the entire fight that continued from morning till evening, the disciple was completely absorbed in the fight. He fought in such a manner that the opponent was safeguarded; he also safeguarded himself from defeat. This demonstrates his quality of concentration.

Sirshree: The seventh quality demonstrated through this bout is that of contemplation.

One should first contemplate on the positive aspects of anything, and then contemplate on the negative aspects. If one contemplates on the negative aspects first, then the positive aspects lose their importance. But when one contemplates on the positive aspects first, the negative aspects do not worry him to that extent.

When the disciple heard about the bout, he first felt compassion for the opponent in spite of the fact that the opponent was an expert wrestler. He didn't become anxious or fearful for his own safety. As a result, he could play the bout with equanimity and ultimately attain higher wisdom from the guru.

Had he become worried about his own safety first, he wouldn't have been able to maintain equanimity throughout the bout and would have lost it.

Seeker A: Right. Quality of our contemplation can improve if we focus on the positive aspects first.

Sirshree: Yes. If someone sees thorns first instead of the flower, he will ignore the beauty of the flower. Instead, if he looks at the beautiful flowers in the beginning and then looks at the thorns, then he understands that the thorns are meant for protecting the beautiful flowers. Hence, we should also contemplate considering the positive aspects first.

In fact, the problems that we face in life help us to become strong. A tree that grows without facing any storms in life, gets uprooted even with the slightest of storms. The tree that faces many storms, develops strong roots. When such a tree grows, no storm can uproot it.

When one inculcates these qualities within oneself, one's body-mind gets prepared to hold the experience of the Self and helps it express the infinite potential of the Self.

14
Common Mistakes of the Disciple

Seeker B: What mistakes can a seeker of truth commit which could delay his search for the truth?

Sirshree: Let's discuss some of the common mistakes. The first mistake is to use the knowledge he has acquired from the guru against the guru himself.

Seeker B: I didn't get you. Can you please elaborate?

Sirshree: Let's consider a disciple attends a spiritual congregation after a long break. When he meets the guru, the guru questions him about his absence. The disciple replies, "Everything happens as per God's will. Nothing is in my hands. It is you, who gave me this understanding. Perhaps, God was graceful on me when I attended the discourses last time. But, it's no longer the case now. Let's see… when God wills… I will be brought back here!"

What kind of reply is this? Doesn't the guru know about his

own teachings? Doesn't he know that everything happens as per God's will?

The guru knows everything, and yet when he questions the disciple, it means there is some serious reason behind it. The guru can use the same logic and say, "The question is also being asked by God's will."

The disciple needs to understand that he is yet to complete his journey of truth and needs further guidance from the guru, instead of quoting an excuse of God's will for not turning up.

Seeker A: That's right. If a seeker is not deceit-free, he may try to deceive the guru. That could be a mistake that he may commit.

Sirshree: Yes, deceit could be the second mistake a disciple commits. On the path of truth, never exaggerate, understate, or hide certain aspects from the guru to suit your convenience. By engaging in deceit, you strengthen your contrast mind and the contrast mind further poses hurdles in attaining your goal. Thus, you hamper your own growth in turn. Hence, always be deceit-free with the guru. If you have any doubts, clarify them with him. Don't bother about what others might think about you. You will then derive maximum benefit from the presence of the guru.

Seeker B: The other day, I was tired after the day's work. My mother asked me to help her with her household chores. I avoided it by justifying that God doesn't want me to assist her now. God would rather want to relax through my body-mind for some time. After some time, I realized that I had misused higher wisdom for the lower purpose in favor of my tendencies to remain in my comfort zone. I am sorry about it.

Sirshree: Yes. This could be the third mistake a disciple commits – to misuse higher wisdom for lower and unworthy purposes. He uses the prolific words spoken by the guru while indulging in gossip and cheap talk.

Imagine that one day you come across Aladdin's magic lamp. You rub the lamp and a genie emerges, ready to fulfil whatever wish you make. While the genie is capable of granting you just about *any* wish, if you make him sweep your house, do you realize the folly you'd be making?! He could have made a huge mansion for you and yet you utilise your fortune for such a lowly trivial task! You are not only under-utilizing its potential, but also misusing it.

When words that hold the power to attain the ultimate goal of life, are used in jokes and cheap talk, it is like making a genie sweep your house. This ultimate wisdom has the potential to liberate you of all the problems in your life. It can make your life simple, spontaneous and straightforward. Your life can be full of bliss and peace.

Seeker B: Thanks for this guidance. I will ensure that I refrain from misusing the wisdom, and sincerely use it instead for my spiritual growth. Next time, when my tendencies instigate me to work in their favor, I won't do it.

Sirshree: Good. The fourth mistake could be to misunderstand the guru's intentions when he is being strict or candidly hurtful.

While walking on the path of the ultimate truth, it's possible that the guru might have to resort to taking stern measures with you. He may use harsh words, become strict with you, or even create deliberate challenges for you. At such times, understand that whatever the guru's actions may be, his pure intention is solely for your own growth. If he is deliberately planting challenges in your path, it is to rid you of your vanity, break your tendencies, discipline your mind and unfold your latent potential.

The guru won't think twice before using harsh words if it is required to propel you towards your goal. Zen masters are known to even use wooden sticks to chide their disciples! The guru can command a disciple to accomplish tasks that the latter might have never expected or imagined, but all that is only meant to annihilate his ego and help him grow.

If the disciple doubts the guru's intentions and feels hurt by his actions, he needs to remind himself that his ego is making him feel so and is obstructing his progress. At such times, the disciple might even blame the guru for being egoistic or arrogant in making him do certain things. In such delicate moments, it is important to have complete and unflinching faith on the guru, his words and actions.

The guru works like a coppersmith. The coppersmith holds the utensil with one hand and strikes the utensil with the other to mould it into perfect shape. The guru also supports the disciple with one hand when he strikes him with the other, to turn him into the perfect receptacle for the ultimate wisdom. Sometimes the guru hurts him, lovingly explains to him, disciplines him, commands him to abide by certain instructions, or even expresses disappointment at him. He does whatever it takes, out of pure compassion for the disciple, to make sure that he progresses on his path.

Seeker A: Once when apparently it wasn't even my fault, you had asked me to seek forgiveness from my colleague and wholeheartedly forgive him. My mind had complained that it's very easy for you to preach; it's difficult for me to practice. But somehow, by grace, I had faith on you and your teachings. I followed your instructions and found that my mind got rid of those hateful thoughts and I felt peaceful. I realized that sincerely following your instructions was in my favor only.

Sirshree: Good. Yes, what you just shared brings out the fifth mistake a disciple may commit. The disciple may follow what his mind says, instead of the instructions of the guru.

When the guru asks him, "Why haven't you been attending the discourse sessions?", the disciple replies, "You are truly a great master and I feel I have learnt everything I wanted from you. I have far less stress, sorrows and problems in life now and I feel my mind has been freed of its vacillations. Whatever you have taught me has greatly benefitted me and shall continue to do so all my life. The wisdom you have blessed me with, has already put everything in my life in its right place, and I no longer feel the need to continue to learn. I have understood and assimilated everything I will ever need."

The guru tries to explain him that the knowledge he has acquired so far is far from complete and there is much more that he needs to know and understand. The disciple however insists that he does not need to continue. He fails to understand that if the very same guru, who bestowed the wisdom that is having such a positive effect in his life, is now asking him to continue to take lessons, there has to be something important that he is missing, that he still hasn't learnt. Such a person is in reality a disciple of his own mind, not the guru. He finds it easy to discard even the guru's behest. Hence, it is important to not let the mind be your spiritual guide.

Seeker A: I will always keep this in mind.

Sirshree: The sixth mistake one can make is when one fails to understand why the guru takes his words back.

Based on the current state of mind, understanding and requirement of a disciple, the guru conveys certain ideas, instructions or explanation to him. Later, when the purpose of those words or instructions is complete, the guru takes them back. The disciple finds it difficult to give up those words and instructions that have greatly helped him overcome his challenges.

The guru then explains, "The words, instructions and explanations that were given to you, have helped you arrive at the current state. It's now time to keep those words and instructions aside as they have fulfilled their purpose and receive new teachings to progress on the further leg of your journey."

Seeker B: Can you please elaborate why this is required?

Sirshree: Okay. Let's understand it with the help of an example:

Consider a child who is afraid of the dark. You give him a talisman and ask him to wear it every time he feels afraid. The child follows this and finds that he can overcome his fear every time he wears it.

When he grows up, you ask him for the talisman, now that he is ready for higher understanding. But he refuses to return it and tells you, "This talisman has helped me get over my fear of darkness! It has greatly benefitted me; I can never give it up!"

You explain, "The talisman was only an instrument that helped you in that particular phase of life. Now, you have conquered fear. You don't need the talisman anymore." But he refuses to let go of it. Instead he hands it over to his son, who is also afraid of the dark! Ironically, the very illusion that you are trying to free the person from, is being propagated further by him!

In spirituality too, many people are stuck with talismans, ash and other things that are only pseudo-spiritual. People are being misled to believe that such things are the true sources of happiness and prosperity. A true guru never encourages such beliefs and takes away everything that you use as a crutch. You have now grown spiritually and are at a much higher plane of understanding. Hence, the guru wants to introduce you to the ultimate wisdom, the final truth that is beyond all beliefs and superstitions, at the apex of all spiritual teachings.

The way the child resisted returning the talisman, the disciple refuses to return the earlier instructions received from the guru. Instead of looking at the short term benefit, have faith that whatever the guru does, is with consideration for your future growth. Hence, don't resist it. After all, it is the guru who is asking you back for his own earlier instructions, so that he can give you something that is more relevant for you now.

Seeker B: Right. I now understand it. Thanks for the guidance!

15
Same Questions, Changing Answers

Seeker B: Why does the guru change his answers to the same question at different times? Doesn't he remember what he has answered earlier?

Sirshree: Answers provided in spirituality change depending on the level of receptivity of the one who is questioning. If a beginner asks, "Can I attain Self-realization, he will be told, "Yes, you can." It is essential to open his mind to the possibility, which is his very birth right.

If someone who has progressed on the path to some extent asks the same question, he'll be told, "Till today, no person has ever been Self-realized." An assumed personality can never attain Self-realization. The "I" that wants it can never attain it. This "I" is the mind trying to seek that experience. This "I" is unreal, it's just a notion. The false "I" can never attain it, and the real "I" doesn't need it, for the real "I" is constantly real-I-zing it!

When an advanced seeker asks whether Self-realization can be attained, he will be told, "There is no question of 'attaining' Self-realization. In truth, Self-realizing alone is going on. That is the sole definitive truth of all existence." Everything that is happening is merely serving the Self to realize its own presence. The world serves as a mirror for Self-knowing.

Seeker A: Right. It's awesome how answers can change depending on where the seeker is in his journey. Are there any other instances where answers can change?

Sirshree: Many! Take the aspect of how a seeker relates to the Guru. The seeker's definition of the Guru changes as he progresses on his journey. Although, the guru only sees the essential Self in the seeker, the novice seeker can't fathom the formless presence of the Self in the guru. Hence, the guru respects his viewpoint and behaves accordingly.

Initially, when the seeker assumes himself as well as the guru to be individuals, the guru interacts with him accordingly. He guides the seeker in terms of the seeker's present understanding.

Gradually, as the seeker gains recognition of the experience of the Self and abides in it, he begins to see the same Self in the body-mind of the guru. The guru then guides him from the standpoint of pure consciousness.

Seeker B: I would have never ever imagined that one question can have so many different answers. I now realize how my perspective was limited. There is a need for such different answers; hence they are given.

Sirshree: When the guru answers a disciple's question, the answer comes straight from Consciousness itself. The answers are not scripted; neither are they prepared. They occur to the guru naturally and spontaneously. Hence, that's the best answer for the disciple and is perfectly fitting for his needs of the time.

If the guru senses that the disciple is not trustworthy, he may even hold back his guidance or instructions as they would prove to be futile. Someone who isn't ready for a deeper and profound answer is given a superficial and simplistic one, to begin with. If such a person were to compare the answer he has received with that received by others, he is bound to get confused. For this reason, truth seekers are made to take a solemn pledge that they wouldn't discuss, compare or even share the knowledge and answers they receive.

Seeker A: Why does the guru create new vocabulary? Why can't he use the traditional words from ancient scriptures?

Sirshree: When the seeker first approaches the guru, his mind is occupied with prevalent vocabulary that holds conventional meaning. If the guru also uses the same traditional words like "spirit", "luck", "fate", or "destiny", the seeker will interpret them in their preconceived ways and derive the same old meaning. The purpose of words from the guru is to catapult the seeker beyond the realm of words and thoughts into pure consciousness. This can't happen if the seeker is latching onto preconceived meanings. He won't decipher the intended meaning out of them. Therefore, the guru redefines these words in the form of a new vocabulary so that the seeker can be freed from his prevalent knowledge as well as ignorance.

Seeker A: Can you please elaborate with an example?

Sirshree: Consider the word "witnesser." When you view the world, the world becomes the object and the eye, the observer. When the mind employs the eye to know things, the eye becomes the object and the mind the knower. However, when the mind itself becomes the object, your true Self is awakened. The Self is observing and knowing the mind and its world, but that is not the ultimate goal. The ultimate goal is that the Self should witness itself while witnessing everything else. Hence, the new word "Self-witnesser" was coined for the Self. It would be impossible for the tongue to taste itself. However, the same is possible for the Self-witnesser by employing the body-mind as the medium. The way an eye uses the mirror as a medium to see itself, the Self uses the body-mind as a mirror to know, to witness, to experience itself subjectively.

Knowing the mind, and knowing *about* the mind are two different things. To know about the mind, one can use one's mind. However, for knowing the mind, you have to detach yourself from your mind and be the one who you truly are, your true Self. The enlightened master guides you to become a detached witnesser and be on your true Self.

In the absence of this understanding, people make the mistake of using their mind to know their mind. This ignorance makes them vulnerable to fraudulent self-proclaimed gurus who convey the wrong meaning of "witnesser". As a result, the sincere seeker of truth engages himself in witnessing everything else except his true Self and goes astray from the ultimate truth. When a true guru enters his life, he convinces the seeker that the truth is beyond what is knowable and he need not seek it outside. Thus, he immerses within to experientially witness his true being.

16
Teaching, Training and Testing

Seeker A: As I go through this journey, I am observing life is throwing up extremely challenging situations. I am being put to test more and more severely and I tend to resist them out of fear. When things don't go as I've planned, I get angry and even set blame on others. When I fail to complete my tasks on time, I get anxious about losing my credibility. When others criticize my work, I feel demoralized. How do I move ahead in the face of such testing situations?

Sirshree: When a seeker of truth starts his journey of truth and faces testing situations, he often questions – how should he move ahead in the face of such increasingly severe testing? Firstly, you need to understand the concept of testing. Unfortunately, you have formed a very scary perception of the idea of *testing*. It has become something undesirable and terrifying for you. To begin with, you need to change this perception.

Let's understand what testing is with help of an example:

Imagine that you want to become an artist who paints pictures.

You are trying to learn the art and in the process, you make a painting. You show it proudly to your family. Your family members cheer you up, "Wow! This is really great work! You are such a great painter!"

Honestly speaking, the truth is that you are a novice and your painting is of average quality. Your skills are still at a preliminary stage. There are still many shortcomings in your work. Your lines need to get sharper and the brushwork needs to get better. You need to know the various shades of colors and their mixtures.

While you are working on improving your skills, a guest who happens to be an expert painter visits your home. He sees your paintings and says, "This is such a poor work!" He goes on to give a very candid feedback about all the fallacies in your work and how you need to be better with your colors and brush strokes.

Now, since the guest's visit, you are more aware of how your brush moves. Your hands and eyes feel strained when you work. You begin doing hand exercises to make it steady, to improve your line-work and brushwork. Would you call all this as "testing"? Isn't all this a preparation for becoming a better artist? Wouldn't it be more accurate to call this "training" rather than a "testing"?

You could always continue to call it a testing situation and take it as a torture. But you should understand that it's a preparation, it's training. The greater an artist you want to become, the more intense training you have to undergo.

In the beginning, you may find the training a little trying. But gradually with time, you will notice that your skills are getting honed, and you will start enjoying them because they foster creativity.

As you gain mastery in painting, you are introduced to higher lessons, which are obviously tougher than the preceding ones. You get to understand the subtleties of the art. If the lessons don't get tougher, you will always remain the novice that you are today.

Testing seems torturous only in the beginning. With time however, they cease to be so and you learn to welcome them and let them be an opportunity for you to express your creativity.

Replace the word *testing* with *training* or *teaching*. This will alleviate the fear of the word *testing* that you have held in your mind. If you are a student of painting, there is nothing wrong or worrisome about undergoing training.

Seeker A: Thanks for this guidance. I now see that I was perceiving these circumstances wrongly. What you have explained is making it clear why testing situations occur in our life. I need to consider them as an opportunity for teaching and training.

Sirshree: At this stage of your journey, it is quite natural for you to feel fearful of testing. However, know that this won't persist because with every passing day, your mastery grows and your *testing* becomes *teaching* and *training*. A time will come when none of this will affect you. In fact, you will start enjoying it.

People abandon the path of spirituality for the fear of being tested and challenged. That is the greatest misfortune! Be perseverant and change your perspective of looking at such testing. It isn't a "test" at all, it is a "taste", and it is very *tasty!* Testing, training, teaching.. all are very tasty! You need to develop the taste for it, as it comes only to unleash your true potential.

Seeker B: But what should I do when I am subjected to too many such situations at the same time? How should I look at them?

Sirshree: When you appear for an exam, you come to know about your weak areas. Similarly, some incidents that occur in life are testing situations, which let us evaluate the extent to which we have assimilated the teachings. We need to get rid of ignorance and gain wisdom in those weak areas.

Before we attain the ultimate truth and stabilize in that experience, we are subjected to extensive testing to prepare for it. Often, it so happens that some testings turn out to be tougher than others. Let's say on a Sunday afternoon, when you really feel tired and sleepy, some guests arrive and you have to attend to them. While you are doing that, the phone rings and while you are speaking on the phone, someone is incessantly barraging you with questions. What a great testing that would be!

In such times, when you feel that the testing is getting too much for you and that you can't handle it anymore, call it as "training" and tell yourself, "This is the highest training. It is grace that I am being subjected to such training for my own growth."

Seeker B: What difference does it make? I will have to still face those situations.

Sirshree: When you face them as testing, you will sense them with a negative undertone. Whereas when you consider them as training, you will shift to a positive frame of mind. You will then tell yourself, "I am undergoing severe training to prepare for my eventual supreme state of being." You have either consciously or unconsciously prayed for the manifestation of the supreme state of being in your life, and for that reason you have to undergo these testing situations.

You may refer to single incidents as testing situations. And when the testing gets tougher, when incidents occur in multitudes, when things go out of control, then you may refer to that phase as "training". However tough it may be, the training is imperative to train your body, mind and intellect so that the Self can experience and express its divine qualities like love, joy, peace, courage, confidence, compassion, and creativity through your body-mind.

Consider a 10 watt bulb. If a current higher than the specification were to flow through the circuit, it would blow the fuse off, damaging the bulb. One would need to bump up the voltage to endure the higher current. Likewise, for the body to become instrumental for the experience and expression of the all-powerful and awakened Self, it has to be prepared and made worthy in all aspects by subjecting it to persistent teaching, testing and training.

Seeker B: Can you please elaborate?

Sirshree: In the game of snakes and ladders, a ladder takes you higher and a snake pulls you down. Likewise, life, the powerful teacher, brings about setbacks, frustrations, challenges, obstacles or struggles in your life. These are the weak areas where your inherent tendencies try to pull you back to your old conditioned ways of living. They distract you from your path and don't let you progress.

These seemingly testing situations you view negatively are actually the results of your higher thoughts for growth, for realizing your innate potential. If you consider them as an opportunity for training and gain wisdom, develop new qualities, then you convert these so-called snakes into ladders of growth. They serve you as an elevating springboard to progress further.

With this understanding, when you are in the midst of struggle, remember the teaching, training and testing triad. Instead of getting mired by the illusory attractions and distractions of the world, shift your focus to higher consciousness, immerse yourself in devotion. What you focus on, multiplies in your life. If you focus on illusions and struggle, they will multiply. If you focus on the truth, it will multiply. Thus, with this higher perspective, you can learn the art of converting every snake that you encounter on your path into a ladder and ultimately reach your final goal smoothly, peacefully and effortlessly.

Seeker B: Gratitude to you! Thanks for all your guidance.

Addendum
The Significance of Guru Purnima

Having read through the profound answers that unravel the essence of the Guru and his role in our lives, let us now understand the significance of *Guru Purnima*.

By tradition, on this day, every disciple, irrespective of his location, tries to visit his guru. This day is a great opportunity to pay respect to the guru, seek his blessings and benefit from his presence. It is a memorable day for disciples, devotees and truth-seekers alike.

Seekers express their love, faith, devotion and gratitude for the guru. They spend the day commending the guru, paying obeisance by dancing, singing hymns of wonderment about how their lives have been transformed by the benevolent light of grace of the guru. Some devote their time in altruistic service, others offer gifts to people. Some express their love in the form of tears, whereas some others in the form of joyous laughter.

Ardent and devout disciples always remember their guru in their heart. However, those seekers, who get caught up in the woes of earthly responsibilities, often keep putting off meeting the guru. This day makes it an inevitable pretext by tradition to do receive the presence of the guru. If it weren't for this day, disciples would keep putting it off until their last breath, which is when they will finally feel the urge to see their guru. To avoid this, it has been made a tradition to meet your guru at least once a year, on the occasion of Guru Purnima.

Guru Purnima – in commemoration of Guru Vyasa

Guru Purnima, also called as Vyasa Purnima, is celebrated in the memory of Guru Vyasa. Guru Vyasa is credited with elaborating the primordial single *Veda* into its canonical parts. The Veda is the greatest source of knowledge in scriptural form and splitting it into comprehensible parts has helped people understand it better. For having achieved this great feat, Guru Vyasa is also known as Veda Vyasa, the elaborator of the Vedas.

Another profound undertaking of Guru Vyasa is the scripting of the great Indian epic, the *Mahabharata*. It's the great mythological epic that was written thousands of years ago. Even today, thousands of years since its inception, this scripture still continues to benefit people. This is essentially because the characters portrayed in the Mahabharata represent human behavior patterns that function within each one of us. You will find that every person you know is similar to some character of the Mahabharata.

Let's consider some examples:

- You will find people like Bhishma, who owing to a pledge of theirs, have to suffer great hardships.
- The world is replete with people like the egoistic Duryodhana, who are burning in the fire of humiliation and are the cause of great sorrow to everyone around them.

- You will find fathers like Dhritarashtra, whose blind love for their children spoils them.

- You will find great scholars like Dronacharya and Kripacharya, who in spite of being very wise and knowledgeable, are compelled to support the unvirtuous.

- There are people like Gandhari, who in spite of having eyesight, chose to blindfold herself out of sheer misbelief and illusions.

- There are people like Dushasana, Karna and Ashwathama, who although brave and virtuous themselves, had to suffer hardships for being in bad company.

- You will find people like Yudhishthira, who although righteous and honorable at heart, have vices like gambling, that put them on the path to ruin.

- Then there are people like Draupadi, who couldn't bring herself to mind her tongue and eventually caused a great war.

- There are people like Bhima, who believe in the use of brute force in every situation.

- Some people are like Arjuna, who under the false pretext of knowledge, want to shy away from their duties.

- There are also few like Lord Krishna, who are guiding people in realizing their true Self and blessing them with the ultimate wisdom. The earth has never been completely devoid of enlightened and Self-established souls.

Humankind has been blessed ever since its earliest times. Every sincere seeker of truth eventually finds a Krishna, who himself summons his disciple and absolves him. The Gita is the most important part of the Mahabharata and its profundity hardly needs any proof.

Symbolism of Guru Purnima

Guru Purnima is a day that symbolizes the giving of eternal wisdom. It is a day to celebrate the wisdom that the guru has blessed us with and express our gratitude for it. It's also a full moon night, symbolizing the guru leading his disciples out of the darkness of ignorance into the light of wisdom. This wisdom, that you acquire during your life on earth, benefits you even hereafter. You get rid of the fear of your own death as well as the death of your loved ones.

On this day, above all the offerings, the greatest offering that the guru expects from his disciples is that of the disciple's comparing, judging contrast mind. The contrast mind is the greatest hurdle on the path of Self-realization.

By bestowing the ultimate wisdom, the guru annihilates your contrast mind, sets you free from fears, beliefs and superstitions to progress on your journey of the ultimate truth. This, in a way, is symbolically a rebirth, because from that point onwards, you lead a new life with a fresh new perspective.

Takeaways from Guru Purnima

This day can open up many possibilities in the disciple's life.

1. Some word or anecdote spoken by the guru could penetrate your understanding like an arrow and precipitate your freedom from illusions. That moment could be a birth of a new you, free from all bondages and sorrows.

2. You could receive a book as a *Prasad* (a gift), reading which could rekindle the wisdom the guru has bestowed upon you.

3. Your interaction with other disciples can renew your love and yearning for the truth.

4. You might feel an urge to express gratitude for the guru's grace and benevolence in the form of a prayer or a hymn, which could change the direction and state of your life.

5. Someone else's fearlessness about life and death could inspire you to acquire the same and absolve yourself of the vicious cycle.

6. The overall atmosphere is conducive for spiritual growth. You feel connected with your true Self and revitalize your quest for the truth.

Even if any one of the above possibilities materializes in your life, this day can be considered fruitful. With this wisdom, you will attain your true Self. You will be immersed in the feeling of benevolence and gratitude, the price of which can't be matched by any of the material possessions and pleasures of the world. Life will become a celebration of the truth in itself!

■ ■ ■

You can send your opinion or feedback on this book to :

Tej Gyan Foundation, Pimpri Colony, P. O. Box 25,
Pimpri, Pune – 411017 (Maharashtra), INDIA
email : mail@tejgyan.com

Write for Us

We welcome writers, translators and editors to join our team. If you would like to volunteer, please email us at: englishbooks@tejgyan.org or call : +91 90110 10963 or +91 90110 13207

About Sirshree

(Symbol of Acceptance)

Sirshree's spiritual quest which began during his childhood, led him on a journey through various schools of thought and meditation practices. His overpowering desire to attain the truth made him relinquish his teaching job. After a long period of contemplation, his spiritual quest culminated in the attainment of the ultimate truth. Sirshree says, **"All paths that lead to the truth begin differently, but end in the same way—with understanding. Understanding is the whole thing. Listening to this understanding is enough to attain the truth."**

Sirshree is the author of several spiritual books. His books have been translated in more than 10 languages and published by leading publishers such as Penguin and Hay House. He is the founder of Tej Gyan Foundation, a not-for-profit organization committed to raising mass consciousness by spreading "Happy Thoughts" with branches in the United States, India, Europe and Asia-Pacific. Sirshree's retreats have transformed the lives of thousands and his teachings have inspired various social initiatives for raising global consciousness.

His works include more than 100 books and 3000 discourses. Various luminaries and celebrities such as His Holiness the Dalai Lama, publishers Mr. Reid Tracy and Ms. Tami Simon and yoga master Dr. B. K. S Iyengar have released Sirshree's books and lauded his work. 'The Source' book series, authored by Sirshree, has sold more than 10 million copies in 5 years. His book *The Warrior's Mirror*, published by Penguin, was featured in the Limca Book of Records for being released on the same day in 11 languages.

Tejgyan... The Road Ahead

What is Tejgyan?

Tejgyan is the existential wisdom of the ultimate truth, which is beyond duality. In today's world, there are people who feel disharmony and are desperately trying to achieve balance in an unpredictable life. Tejgyan helps them in harmonizing with their true nature, the Self, thereby restoring balance in all aspects of their life.

And then there are those who are successful but feel a sense of emptiness or void within. Tejgyan provides them fulfillment and helps them to embark on a journey towards self-realization. There are others who feel lost and are seeking the meaning of life. Tejgyan helps them to realize the true purpose of human life.

All this is possible with Tejgyan due to a very simple reason. The experience of the ultimate truth is always available. The direct experience of this truth is possible provided the right method is known. Tejgyan is that method, that understanding. At Tej Gyan Foundation, Sirshree imparts this understanding through a System for Wisdom – a series of retreats that guides participants step by step

Magic of Awakening Retreat

Magic of Awakening is the flagship self-realization retreat offered by Tej Gyan Foundation The retreat is conducted in two languages – Hindi and English. The teachings of the retreat are non-denominational (secular).

This residential retreat is held for 3-5 days at the foundation's MaNaN Ashram amidst the glory of mountains and the pristine nature. This ashram is located at the outskirts of the city of Pune in India, and is well connected by air, road and rail. The retreat is also held at other centres of Tej Gyan Foundation across the world.

Participate in the *Magic of Awakening* retreat to attain ageless wisdom through a unique simple 'System for Wisdom' so that you can:

1. Live from pure and still presence allowing the natural qualities of consciousness, viz. peace, love, joy, compassion, abundance and creativity to manifest.

2. Acquire simple tools to use in everyday life which help quieten the chattering mind, revealing your true nature.

3. Get practical techniques to access pure presence at will and connect to the source of all answers (the inner guru).

4. Discover missing links in practices of meditation *(dhyana)*, action *(karma)*, wisdom *(gyana)* and devotion *(bhakti)*.

5. Understand the nature of your body-mind mechanism to attain freedom from tendencies and patterns.

6. Learn practical methods to shift from mind-centred living to consciousness-centred living.

For retreats contact +919921008060 or email: mail@tejgyan.com

A Mini retreat is also conducted, especially for teens (14-17 years) during summer and winter vacations

MaNaN Ashram

Survey No. 43, Sanas Nagar, Nandoshi gaon, Kirkatwadi Phata, Sinhagad Road, Dist. Pune 411024, Maharashtra, India.

About Tej Gyan Foundation

Tej Gyan Foundation (TGF) was established with the mission of creating a highly evolved society through all-round self development of every individual that transforms all the facets of his/her life. It is a non-profit organization founded on the teachings of Sirshree. The foundation has received the ISO certification (ISO 9001:2015) for its system of imparting wisdom. It has centres all across India as well as in other countries. The motto of Tej Gyan Foundation is 'Happy Thoughts'.

TGF is creating a highly evolved society through:

- Tejgyan Programs (Retreats, Courses, Television and Radio Programs, Podcasts)

- Tejgyan Products (Books, Tapes, Audio/Video CDs)

- Tejgyan Projects (Value Education, Women Empowerment, Peace Initiatives)

TGF undertakes projects to elevate the level of consciousness among students, youth, women, senior citizens, teachers, doctors, leaders, organizations, police force, prisoners, etc.

Now you can register online for the following retreats

Maha Aasmani Niwasi Shivir
(5 Days Residential Retreat in Hindi)

Magic of Awakening Retreat
(3 Days Residential Retreat In English)

Mini Maha Aasmani Shivir
3 Days (Residential) Retreat for Teens

www.tejgyan.org

Books can be delivered at your doorstep by registered post or courier. You can request for the same through postal money order or pay by VPP. Please send the money order to either of the following two addresses:

WOW Publishings Pvt. Ltd.

1. Registered Office: E-4, Vaibhav Nagar, Near Tapovan Mandir, Pimpri, Pune 411017.

2. Post Box No. 36, Pimpri Colony Post Office, Pimpri, Pune 411017

Phone No. : 9011013210 / 9623457873

You can also order your copy at the online store:

www.gethappythoughts.org

*Free Shipping plus 10% Discount on purchases above Rs. 300/-.

For further details contact:

Tejgyan Global Foundation

Registered Office:
Happy Thoughts Building, Vikrant Complex, Near Tapovan Mandir, Pimpri, Pune 411017, Maharashtra, India.
Contact No: 020-27411240, 27412576
Email: mail@tejgyan.com

MaNaN Ashram:
Survey No. 43, Sanas Nagar, Nandoshi gaon, Kirkatwadi Phata, Sinhagad Road, Tal. Haveli, Dist. Pune 411024, Maharashtra, India.
Contact No: 992100 8060.

Hyderabad: 9885558100, **Bangalore:** 9880412588,

Delhi: 9891059875, **Nashik:** 9326967980, **Mumbai:** 9373440985

For accessing our unique 'System for Wisdom' from self-help to self-realization, please follow us on:

	Website	www.tejgyan.org
YouTube	Video Channel	www.youtube.com/tejgyan For Q&A videos: http://goo.gl/YA81DQ
facebook	Social networking	www.facebook.com/tejgyan
twitter	Social networking	www.twitter.com/sirshree
	Internet Radio	http://www.tejgyan.org/internetradio.aspx

Online Shopping
www.gethappythoughts.org

Pray for World Peace along with thousands of others at 09:09 a.m. and p.m. every day

www.ingramcontent.com/pod-product-compliance
Lightning Source LLC
LaVergne TN
LVHW041845070526
838199LV00045BA/1448